Tony,

I wish you
great health, hap
and a success y

HOPE

HOPE

Finding the Path toward
Happiness, Opportunity,
Prosperity, and Enjoyment

WANNY HUYNH
with Jody Mabry

BEAVER'S
POND
PRESS

ISBN 13: 978-1-59298-765-8

Library of Congress Catalog Number: 2016908607

Printed in the United States of America
First Printing: 2016
20   19   18   17   16   5   4   3   2   1

Cover and interior design by James Monroe Design, LLC.

Beaver's Pond Press, Inc.
7108 Ohms Lane
Edina, MN 55439–2129
(952) 829-8818
www.BeaversPondPress.com

Dedication

Throughout much of my life I have experienced struggles. Whether it was growing up in poverty and being taken into child slavery, emigrating to a new country, or getting through my personal struggles and conflicts, I have found that anyone can overcome the obstacles in their life.

To me, it is not failure that defines us but rather the blocks we stumble over and manage to get past. There are very few people who are able to do this without the help of others—maybe for you, it's your parents, friends, siblings, or a total stranger; there is good everywhere, and you should never forget that. In part I dedicate this book to those people who help others through their struggles. Because you must remember that they have struggles of their own.

Secondly, this book is dedicated to you, the reader. You are reading this book because you have struggles you wish to overcome. Coming to the realization that you are struggling, and need help is the first, and most important step to overcoming your obstacles and achieving your dreams. I did not do it alone, although at times I was too stubborn or prideful to admit I needed help. It wasn't until I acknowledged to myself that I needed to change that things got better. I had to acknowledge that despite my past difficulties, I was responsible for my own actions, and simply, I needed to fix myself to achieve my dreams.

We all have it in us to do this. So, this book is dedicated to your future self—the one who achieved your dreams!

Contents

CHAPTER 1

Beginnings

Human progress is neither automatic nor inevitable.
Every step toward the goal of justice requires sacrifice,
suffering, and struggle; the tireless exertions and passionate
concern of dedicated individuals.

—MARTIN LUTHER KING JR.

I was born and lived in Bac Lieu, just south of Saigon, Vietnam, until I was eight years old. To Americans, the area would have been more commonly known as the Mekong Delta from the Vietnam War, which, while officially over when I was a child, still brewed within the confines of the surrounding jungles. When I say we lived in Bac Lieu, I mean our village was about a thirty-minute motorcycle ride from Bac Lieu. So the luxuries, which would have existed in a city like Bac Lieu, were unknown to me. The name of our village was Prey Chop. Our home was nothing more than a shack with mud bricks for walls and banana leaves for the roof. We had no running water, we had no electricity, and our village had a single dirt road running through it, surrounded by only a few hundred people.

I can't think of anywhere in America where you would find a dwelling like that unless visiting an American Indian museum or a survivalist.

I don't remember much from the time we spent in the small village of Prey Chop, but I do remember a few things. I attended school until the first grade. My older brother, Wanna, and I would walk to school every day. Like many children, I don't remember learning much in school, as I was too busy daydreaming. Later in life, I would find this both a good and bad attribute, whichever way you wanted to look at it. I'd often think about the afternoon activities, such as playing foosball and buying candy. But the one thing I would probably think about the most was playing marbles. Of all the things I've ever done in my life, the game of marbles was one that came naturally to me. It was something that I could honestly say I had a passion about.

Every day before school, we would shoot marbles in front of the house. I got so good that people would come by and watch me play, and I would compete against other kids in the village. We would play what you call *for keeps*. If you lose the match, you lose your marbles to the winner. For me, it was exciting, as I could always not only grow my marble collection but also improve my playing skills. I had collections upon collections of marbles in our house from all the games I'd won. Twenty years later when I went back to visit, I didn't see them displayed or hear anyone mention where they were. The house we grew up in now belongs to my relatives, who my parents passed it on to when our family left. My display of achievement was no longer there. I'm guessing my nieces or nephews probably lost them all, or they got smart and sold or traded them in for candy. I pick the latter.

Marbles was one of my skills, and later in life, as my family's journey progressed forward, that skill helped feed my family while we were in the refugee camp. You see, the area of the refugee camp where we lived was near the front of a hospital. I would hang out outside the hospital with the other kids playing marbles. Doctors and other people working there would see me. Apparently, they enjoyed watching and took notice of the little kids gathering more marbles every day. Soon they were asking me for lessons. In exchange for me teaching them, they would give me food and water, which I brought back to my family. Without much in the refugee camp, this was a way I could pitch in. I would have been nine years old at the time.

Thinking of the struggles I have had since leaving Prey Chop, it is almost comical, as I don't really consider our everyday life in Vietnam to have been a struggle—that is, until the day we left.

When I was eight years old, my family escaped Vietnam in the middle of the night and journeyed to Cambodia in hopes of getting to Thailand. There were probably about a dozen other people traveling with us when we left. Life was bad, although as a child, I wouldn't have thought or known there was anything better. Between 1975 and 1995, over two million people escaped Vietnam either by boat or by foot, hoping to reach the free world. Out of the two million, only eight hundred thousand made it to the refugee camp. My family was one of the lucky ones.

You could escape Vietnam in three ways. The first, which most tried, was by boat. The problem was that this might be more dangerous than the other two options. You would have to pay someone a lot of money to smuggle you out, and most people failed trying. The Vietcong would intercept your route and kill you on the spot. If you managed to make it out, you still would have to face the pirates who would kill and rob you dry, leaving you to face the open sea. Most people died from dehydration and starvation.

The second option was for a woman to marry an American, usually a soldier. After they were married, her children would be considered American citizens, as well as the woman. Then they could simply leave. This was obviously the easiest way. Yet it wasn't an option for our family.

So we took the last escape, and that was by foot, walking at night along hidden trails, abandoned roads, and a dense, highly dangerous jungle. Despite being in the jungle, we always had the protection of the village around us. But walking through the jungle, we had little protection from the elements, such as deadly snakes and other jungle animals, though that was less of a concern. We were more worried about getting caught by the Vietcong—they are the deadliest of all. They don't give you a warning and tell you to return home. They will either rob, rape, or kill you on the spot. But this was our only option and the risks of escape were worth it.

During the journey, soldiers captured us four times. The first time we were captured, they pretty much took anything of value that we couldn't sneak away while they searched us. The Vietcong took our personal belongings, family photos, and documentation. Luckily, my dad had a connection with some of the commanding officers, and they were willing to bail us out the first time. During our second capture, the soldiers took more personal belongings. By our fourth capture, at the Cambodian border, we had nothing left. That's when the Khmer Rouge soldiers took my brother and me, holding us back, while letting our family go. I don't know if the intention was to hold us for ransom or forever, but for my brother and me, at eight and ten years old, we must have thought we would never see our family again, despite the promises I'm sure my parents gave us.

The soldiers forced my family away, leaving my brother Wanna and me to stay. Of course, once our group had moved on, the soldiers seemed puzzled with what to do with us, as they discussed among themselves while smoking their cheap cigarettes. After a while, they simply let us go. It was common in those days, perhaps even now, for children my age and my brother's age to be accepted into the military, if only to work for the soldiers in a fashion no better than slavery. Considering this, I have to believe the soldiers or a commanding officer may have regretted splitting up a family, which is why we were let go. Either that or my daydreaming was bad enough that they thought I'd be more of a detriment than a value, and I'd cause them to lose all their marbles (excuse the pun). Either way, my brother and I were left alone in an open grassy field of Cambodia; all we had was each other and the T-shirts and shorts on our skinny bodies. I remember it being cold in the middle of the night, and the only plan we could come up with was to continue on the path our family was headed. Scared and shivering, my brother and I continued our journey; the only light that led the way was the full moon above. For two children like my brother and me, we likely didn't make it very far before we became too scared to move on alone, and we made the decision to turn back.

When we arrived back at the checkpoint where we had been originally captured, we were again stopped. Another group of soldiers found their way to the checkpoint shortly after we arrived. One of the leaders of that group saw us, two boys, and he brought us home with him. Not having any sons, he was nice to us, adopting us as his own. He did have two daughters, who were younger than Wanna and I, but wanting sons, we now belonged to him. The soldier treated us well, as if we were his, but his wife was a different story. She wasn't going to accept some other woman's children as her own. In many similar instances, families, especially fathers with daughters, accepted these children more than their own, as was the case between the soldier and my brother and me. So when the husband went out on military duty, the wife would essentially make us work like slaves, what we'd now call child labor. Some of our everyday tasks were to bring water from the well up to the house and carry loads of rice on our backs, and at night, we would have to sleep outside on the ground without a mosquito net. Every morning, we would wake up with tons of red mosquito bites all over our skinny bodies.

I can't remember the names of the couple, but this had been going on for months; the labor and sleeping arrangements were unknown to the husband the entire time. My brother and I were both miserable and likely thought it would never end.

However, as often happens, there was another story unfolding that we knew nothing about and would at some time in the future meet our path. There was a woman, a vendor, who traveled to town, back and forth daily. The house where we lived with the soldier, his wife, and their daughters was next to the house of the vendor's family members. Since the house was along her journey to and from the town, the vendor would often stop to spend the night with her family. One day while visiting her relatives, she noticed these two boys next door in the yard working. When she asked her family who they were, they shrugged and said they didn't know, so the woman continued on her regular activities back and forth to town. Those two boys, Wanna and me, remained on her mind as the woman traveled and worked. But, being after the war, there were thousands of orphaned children everywhere, and it wouldn't have been too strange to see them working for whatever food or shelter they could get. She must have thought this was the case, but still, we were always on her mind. Something wasn't right, yet what could be done?

Meanwhile, our family was living in a nearby town, unwilling to go farther without my brother and me. My mom spent much of her day asking travelers, vendors, and anyone who would listen if they had seen her two boys. She would tell them that she was missing two boys who had been kidnapped by the soldiers. People would claim, "Yeah, we've see the two boys, but first you have to give us some money." Mom, desperate, fell for the story a few times. She would give them money, hoping they would bring us back, but they never would. Finally, after being scammed multiple times, she realized she needed to be much smarter than simply giving people the money without proof. She continued seeking out travelers who came through town, asking if they had seen her two boys, and again, people claimed they had seen us, but when Mom asked the people to describe us to her, none of the descriptions were close. Despite this, she never gave up hope. She always had faith and knew that her two boys were out there some-where, hoping one day to be reunited.

The vendor, while visiting her family one day, couldn't hide her curiosity. With her family knowing nothing of our situation, the woman began talking to my brother and me when she saw us behind the house.

"How are you related to this family?" she asked us. That is when we told her we were not, and we explained that we had been captured and brought there. In fact, we told her our entire situation. It didn't take long for her to realize that despite the problems surrounding postwar Vietnam, this was still an uncommon situation—or at least *she* thought it was. Yet still, there was nothing she could do until several weeks later . . .

The vendor was working and talking with another traveler who mentioned a woman in a nearby town who was looking for two boys. I can only imagine the excitement the woman had when she heard this. The vendor quickly traveled to the town where my family was living. She found my mom, and when she did, she stared at her from a distance. From about ten feet away, she stopped and stared at my mom. Mom recalls thinking, *What is she looking at? Why is she staring at me?* The lady then moved closer to my mom, still making sure to keep a distance as she moved around her, just looking at her. The whole while, Mom watched her, wondering who this woman was and what she was doing.

"You know, you look like one of the boys I've seen."

My mom thought, *Yeah, I've heard that before.* She didn't think much of it.

The woman dismissed my mom's reaction, and then she began to describe the two boys to my mom. "These two boys are about eleven and nine." She went on to describe what we were wearing and how we behaved. But the one thing the vendor mentioned that struck my mom was when she described the youngest son (me). She described the way I squat and the left mole on top of my lips. That's when our mom realized the lady was describing her two boys. So Mom asked, "Can you take me to them?" The lady, of course, said she would.

The husband refused to give us up to my parents; his wife, on the other hand, despised us both and wanted money. So she conceived a plan while her husband was away that she would give us back to our parents for a large sum of money. Our parents said they would do it. So they went back to the town and sold nearly everything they had left and borrowed the rest until they finally had enough.

The husband still refused to give us up for any amount of money, so the only time they could swap us was when he was out on military leave. So one day, when the husband was out on military duty, the wife handed us over. We didn't need to sneak out. Mom just gave the woman the money, and we left. To this day, I wish I knew the whereabouts of the vendor who helped reunite my family. I wish I knew if she was still alive. I owe a deep gratitude to this woman. The only thing I know about this mystery woman is that her first name is Mon-vary.

Now I don't tell this simply as a good story from my past, but rather to introduce you to what I consider one of the most fundamental ways to lead your life in hopes of attaining a better life for yourself and those around you. When I look at this story, I don't see it as my story or even my brother's story. I see this as my mother's story: her strength, her perseverance, but most of all her hope. Hope is what we all have to a degree, something that gives us the willpower to move forward and drive us toward our goals. Hope is the focus of my book. As I like to define it, the path toward happiness, opportunity, prosperity, and enjoyment is HOPE.

As we move forward through this book, I'd like you to reflect on the acronym of HOPE—what it stands for, and how to apply it to your everyday life, like my mom did, to achieve the goals you desire.

CHAPTER 2

Revelations

*The real glory is being knocked to your knees
and then coming back. That's real glory.
That's the essence of it.*

—Vince Lombardi

For everyone, we come to a place where we realize exactly who we are and where we are in life. For me, there are two distinctive times. One I often refer to as the Dollar Tree story, and the other was with my parents. Both stories show a period in my life where I was down and something sparked me toward my calling.

The year 2007 for me was what I would consider one of the lowest points in my life. I was thirty-two years old and living in my parents' basement. I remember sitting in my broken-down Acura Integra in front of Caribou Coffee. While the world around me was busy, and as I watched people walking around, I felt an overwhelming sense of loneliness. I had felt lonely before, but at this moment, for some reason, I felt truly alone. In my pocket was my last dollar bill. I am not talking about the last dollar bill in my pocket. This was literally my last dollar bill. I had no change, nothing in a bank account, no stocks—literally nothing else. I stared at the coffee shop and looked down at my last dollar bill. It was the middle of June. The sun was beating down on me, and the car had no air-conditioning. All I could do was drop the windows to let the outside hot air in. On a hot and muggy day, a cold drink would have hit the spot. But with only a dollar left to my name, I couldn't even afford a cup of ice, let alone a drink. It was then that I asked myself an important question. How can I turn this dollar bill into one million? While staring at the dollar bill, I noticed from the corner of my eye this big green sign. When I looked up, I realized it was a Dollar Tree store sign across the street. Whether I had even noticed the sign prior to then, I can't recall. On any other day, it would have been little more than an everyday sign I dismissed regularly. But something about holding that dollar and seeing that sign prompted me to want to go inside. I didn't know what I was going to do in there or even buy. I couldn't even afford something that was a dollar with tax.

Yet, with this dollar bill in my hand, I walked across the street and walked out with a college-ruled composition notebook. Then I got back in my car. To this day, I think how strange it is that, of all the things I needed—food, shelter, water—it was a notebook I walked out with. Surprisingly, it made perfect sense. Back in my car, I sat for a long time. I wrote on the cover: Journey to Financial Freedom. Then I began asking myself questions. "Why am I not a millionaire? Why am I not successful?" As I wrote those questions in the notebook, the answers just started pouring out of me. It was as if God were giving me a message and doing all the writing through me. I couldn't write my answers down fast enough. At that moment, I began to evaluate myself. "Why am I in this spot?" The answers started flowing through me with so much energy. It was a moment that changed my life. I was completely broke. Yet I sat there writing, completely confident everything would simply work out for me. At that moment, I had no doubt in my mind that, regardless of my current state and that which lay ahead, I would somehow get out of this mess.

That was the day that changed everything. I promised myself that I would never starve again, unless it was by choice. I realized that for me to get out of the mess I was in, I needed to change.

I wrote down these questions:

1. What do I need to do to get myself out of this mess?

2. Who do I have to become?

3. Why am I not a millionaire?

4. What is preventing me from becoming a millionaire?

That was the first step toward my journey to financial freedom. I began to take action. I started to seek out people who went from zero to hero. I wanted to know about people who went from nothing to becoming self-made millionaires and billionaires. I came across such names as Robert Kiyosaki, Brian Tracy, Zig Ziglar, Jim Rohn, Dale Carnegie, Earl Nightingale, and many others. I began to study how they became great in their fields. What were their secrets?

My first stop was the library. I searched out books and audio CDs that could help me to improve myself. I began to use the skills and techniques I had read about, and I implemented them in my daily life.

The second thing I did was to take a true inventory of myself:

1. I'm thirty-two years old and broke.

2. I have no money in the bank.

3. I tend to start something but never finish.

4. I have no role models.

5. I have a lot of dreams, but I don't take action to complete them.

6. I lack practical know-how.

7. I lack resources.

8. I tend to be lazy.

With the list in front of me, I had no excuse but to take action and start working on myself. I listened to audio CDs in the car while I drove to and from work—"Automobile University," as Zig Ziglar calls it. I began to chip away at all the bad things holding me back from being the man I wanted to be.

In the movie *Big Fish*, some kids sneak up to a witch's house to stare into her eye. There's a legend that if you look into the witch's eye, you'll see how you'll die. The kids do it, and when they look into the witch's eye, they all see how they'll pass. The main character, Ed, realizes that if you know how and when you die, you can do anything in between, and regardless of the outcome of those events, they will not kill you, which enables you to go on. Most people fail because they are afraid of the results, but if you take fear out of the equation, your probability of success greatly increases. Ed goes on to have incredible adventures and a great life, all due to the fact that he no longer fears failure or death. This is how I felt in the car that day. Everything seemed to click suddenly, and regardless of failures that I had been experiencing at that time, and despite failures I knew I would later experience, I knew I would achieve my dreams.

Zig Ziglar said, "You are what you are and where you are because of what has gone into your mind. You can change what you are and where you are by changing what goes into your mind."

To be successful in anything, you first have to train your mind. We have to reprogram ourselves to think like the rich people think. To express it in computer language, we have to upgrade our systems. Our old beliefs will have to be replaced with a new way of thinking. We become what we think about.

Throughout time, many wise people have agreed on the principle that we become what we think about. James Allen wrote a groundbreaking book about the power of the mind called *As a Man Thinketh*. There was a time when I thought that for me to become rich and successful, I had to go to school, get a good job, be a doctor or a lawyer, or marry someone rich. But I soon found out that none of that really matters. Many successful people don't have college degrees. Bill Gates was a college dropout, and he's one of the richest men in the world.

The late Jim Rohn once said, "Formal education can earn you a living; self-education can earn you a fortune."

When I was younger, I was looking for ways to make big money. I was willing to try anything. I sold everything from water filters to knives. I failed in all those areas until finally I realized that maybe I wasn't cut out to be a businessman. This is when I joined the corporate world. While working for some of the world's largest companies, I began to hear someone's name all over the place. His name was Robert Kiyosaki. I began to do some digging on him. During that time, his book *Rich Dad Poor Dad* was on the *New York Times* best-seller list. I bought a copy, and after reading his book, it made sense to me that this is how the rich got rich. I told myself that I could do this. The first place I looked to build wealth was in real estate. I knew that this was where the rich held or controlled most of their wealth; Robert Kiyosaki talks about how he became rich investing in real estate. Real estate worked out for a brief moment. In actuality, I failed. But the one thing I could say, as opposed to all things previously in my life, is that I did not fail due to my lack of work. I worked hard. I learned a lot, but the culmination of a bad decision and the housing crisis (horrible timing) hurt me. Yet, as in the movie *Big Fish*, I knew when and how I would die, and this was merely a learning adventure that taught me more about not jumping into a career path with impulsive gusto but rather to focus, learn, and be patient. These would be my personal rules to making educated decisions going forward.

When I was young, my parents taught me that to be successful I had to go to school, get good grades, go to college, and get a good job. It seems like a simple formula, and in fact it is one that works for millions of people. But not everyone is the same. What about those people who have a different gait? What about the artists and entrepreneurs who seek their own rhythm in life and cannot be bound by the limits of a known, simple formula? I knew what my parents wanted, and I knew their plan. But that plan didn't work well for me. I did not have a mentor in my life for the person I was and how I thought. My parents didn't have the resources available to them to help me with this. Their friends were all hard workers who worked for companies. My parents and siblings did the same. Neither my family nor I had entrepreneurial friends to help mentor me. Again, with all my newfound energy, I still felt within me a sense of loneliness. This is when I began to take to heart the advice from all the books I'd been reading. I needed to change myself, and that included to a large degree those I was surrounding myself with. At this time, I developed a mantra for myself: "We become who we hang around with."

I started to surround myself with people who were smarter than I. I read books on people I respected and admired. I began visiting the library more often. Not having any money, I began shopping at Half Price Books. I still do to this day. I even bought books from Goodwill—you can't believe all the books people donate to Goodwill. What a treasure! The next thing I knew, I had my very own library. That's how wealthy people become wealthy and successful—they are always learning and growing. Have you ever wondered why every rich and wealthy family has a study or a library in their house? It's not an accident. It takes them years to get to where they are. They continue learning and growing each and every day.

After the Dollar Tree, I had a path for myself of how to get out of my rut, yet still I did not have the specific goal I was searching for. I had learned how to lay a foundation of improvement for myself and build my knowledge base. I had learned it was okay to fail as long as I can learn from the failure. In my twenties, I'd spent much of my time trying to be the man my parents wanted. I tried to follow their simple formula for life. I even went to school to be a doctor at one point. But I quickly realized I was not cut out for that line of work. Being an accountant wasn't good for me, either, as I was horrendous at math. As I struggled to fulfill what I thought my parents wanted me to do, I missed the big picture of what they truly wanted. They wanted me to be happy. Their dreams of me as a doctor, lawyer, or accountant were not specific to those careers. What they wished for me was the success that usually comes with being a doctor, lawyer, or accountant. Their dream was not for me to succeed in those careers but rather for me to succeed in *my* career—the one I chose. However, at the time, I hadn't figured that out. While I had the beginnings of a game plan for myself, I still did not have the one specific goal I needed.

I was in the kitchen at my parents' house one day when my parents came in. I could tell they wanted to talk to me about something, and while I hadn't figured out how I was going to fully overcome my obstacles, that didn't make me dim-witted. I could tell by the concerned looks on my parents' faces what this conversation was going to be about. We sat down at the table. Both of my parents said to me, "You are in your mid-thirties with no wife and no kids. You're broke. What do you want to do with your life?"

It was simple and to the point, as my parents had often been throughout my life. I looked into their concerned faces, and I could see how much they loved me. But I could also see fear. They thought I was failing at life. That is not an easy feeling for a child to accept from his parents. Throughout my life, I was expected to meet or exceed my parents' expectations. When I didn't, to me, I was a failure to them. That was a turning point for me.

My mom began to share the story of us coming here to America. She shared our struggles and our hardships. After she shared the story, I thought of all the struggles my parents had to go through to bring us to America. I can still recall vividly the experience our family had gone through as bullets and missiles flew over our heads. My mother was carrying my five-month-old sister, while my older cousin, who I called Bong Tee, was carrying my other sister, who was four years old at the time. I remember the adrenaline rush as we sought shelter. Dead bodies of men, women, and children were piled all around us. Bong Tee got weak in the knees, as all of this was happening so fast. We were in a legitimate war zone. This wasn't Hollywood; it was real life. My mom, who was strong willed, took charge, and she yelled for Bong Tee to keep pushing forward. Finally, we found a bunker big enough for all six of us to fit inside. All the while, shrapnel sprayed around us. I couldn't help but think, *Is this how we are going to die?* Shaken and frightened, not sure if we were going to survive, I looked at my mom. She was calm like a true leader would be in a stressful situation. She made quick decisions to keep us alive. This was a life-and-death situation. My mom came through. Her strength and perseverance kept us moving forward. It was a good thing, as the family looked to her for guidance.

Out of nowhere, we heard a loud voice. "My dear! It not safe here; you need to move your family out of this hole."

It was an older gentleman in his sixties who was near the bunker. He pointed to a nearby bunker for us to go. My mom didn't think twice. She quickly gathered everyone, and we all made our way to the nearby bunker, which was no more than twenty yards away. Once we were all safe, we noticed the old gentlemen hop into that same bunker we'd just pulled out of. To this day, I ask myself, *Why did he tell us to move out of that bunker?* Moreover, why did he jump in there? A second after he jumped in, *boom!* A missile struck his bunker. The old gentlemen risked his own life to save ours. God works in mysterious ways. Our family was given another chance in life.

As I looked back and reflected on the struggles and obstacles our family overcame, I realized what was in front of me was just a small bump in the road compared to what our family experienced to get here. I had heard these stories before. My siblings and I could still remember them, and my parents would occasionally share the behind-the-scenes stories children often miss while growing up. Children rarely know the true state of life and the hardships their parents face while raising a household. But even knowing the stories, they are nothing except entertainment until you are older and can appreciate the hardship they faced at that time. At that moment, I began to see the spark of that hardship. So here I was—down, beaten, and broke, yet still better off than my parents had been when we left Vietnam. Why would I let this discourage me from achieving my dreams? Or, better yet, *how could I* let this discourage me from achieving my dreams? It was that realization that enabled me to focus on what I wanted to do in life.

It took me a long time to search and find the answer to this question: *What is it that I am passionate about?* What is it that I want from life? What is my reason to be on this earth? Once I found that purpose, everything seemed to fall into place.

The thing is, I love to tell stories, and speaking was something I could use to share my message. That's when I started reading books. I came across Jack Canfield's *The Success Principles*, and in that book, it was like he spoke to me: "Wanny, if you want to become a speaker, join Toastmasters." So I joined Toastmasters, and I began speaking. More doors opened up for me. I met professional speakers and aspiring speakers. We shared ideas, and they helped to guide me to my goals and my dreams. Through finding my purpose, I was able to find where I wanted to go.

It was in these early stations of my development or transformation that I was able to build the foundation for the rest of my life. By identifying my weaknesses, I was able to determine how to grow and what path I wanted to lead. Had I not written down the honest inventory of who I was, I would have never discovered who I wanted to be. From there, I still experienced failure, yet I was prepared to face it and learn from it. Finally, I did something that I had never previously been able to do. I taught myself how to learn. I engulfed learning as a means of building myself up and reminding myself that I am not the only one who has journeyed down this path. The path is a long journey you start on your own. Every obstacle you pass gives you hope and courage to face the next obstacle until you reach the end, where you finally join the others who trekked the same path.

Chapter 2 Review and Lesson Plan

For you to be successful in any area, you have to change the way you think. I am not saying that you should change the person you are or that you need to become someone else, but you can change by adopting a new way of thinking. Learn how others with the same goal as you have succeeded. How did they do this, how did they behave, and what risks did they have to take?

I needed to change myself. I knew that being my old self wasn't taking me anywhere. Who did I need to become? Once I got a glimpse of the person I wanted to be, I began by acting and playing the part.

You can do it too. Every day, picture the life that you want to live. What would make you happy? What does success look like for you? What does a fulfilling life mean to you? Is having a loving and healthy family a success? If you are already living the life you envision, then congratulations. If you are still seeking out your passion, continue to learn and grow.

Create a life that you want for yourself in your mind, and soon you will begin to live that life.

Activities:

1. Define your goal.

2. Ask yourself these questions:

    • What do I need to do to get myself out of my current situation?

- Who do I have to become to achieve my goal?

- Why have I not already achieved my goal?

- What is preventing me from achieving my goal?

3. Take a true inventory of yourself. Be honest. If you are a procrastinator, then say that. If you are lazy or bad with money, mention that, as well. In this exercise, I would like you to list at least ten things about yourself that hold you back. Try to list things you need to improve on. It is great to know your strengths, but for this exercise, you want to make an honest inventory of what is holding you back in order to move forward.

4. Begin to teach yourself. This does not have to be related to your career path or goals. It helps, of course, but learning is an art. Gathering knowledge can only broaden your life and open you up to opportunities you never knew existed.

5. Research groups or clubs that have similar interests as you. The Internet has a wealth of information on local groups, clubs, and organizations. A quick search will get you in touch with like-minded people. Surround yourself with the people you want to be.

Once you have an evaluation of your true self down on paper, you will begin to see where and how you can start to improve on chasing your dreams.

CHAPTER 3

Reality Check

What we achieve inwardly will change outer reality.

—PLUTARCH

It is one thing to know what we want in life and how we want to achieve those goals. The real obstacle is whether we can be honest with who we are and if it's possible to achieve our goals being the people we are. Most of us need to come to the realization that being who we've been will not get us to where we want to go. That's reminiscent of the quote "The definition of insanity is doing the same thing over and over and expecting a different result." This statement can't be truer. In fact, as I sat in the car outside the Dollar Tree so many years ago, I hadn't yet come to the realization that I truly needed to change me. All my problems, as much as I wanted to blame them on everything else, had one unwavering factor. That factor was me. I didn't always think my "bad luck" was my fault. But as I sat there writing down what I wanted and how I would get there, I came to a revelation (although it wouldn't blossom until years later) that I needed to change me.

The idea that you need to change yourself is a hard reality to face. You, your personality, and who you are is often the only reality you know. You are the only certainty in your life. Everyone around you, including your family and friends, has the ability to surprise and disappoint you. However, you have complete control of your life and what you do, right? I think if you sit back and are honest with yourself, you'll find that this statement is not always true. For example, you know it's not good for you to go to a Chinese buffet and eat five plates of food, right? Not only are you eating way too many calories but you will feel bad and eventually lethargic. Your stomach will ache, and you will regret your decision. We all know this. It is something many of us have done, yet how many of us have done this over and over again? Thomas Jefferson noted in his maxims to do everything in modesty. Eat modestly, spend money modestly, think modestly, but who out there can actually say they do?

I sat there in the car with my two lists in hand. Of those twelve questions and statements, only one of them dug into me. Only the statement *I am lazy* tells you why I was having problems. Of those twelve notes, that statement was my only true reality check. You see, the Dollar Tree story is important because it was one of several times where I realized something was wrong. It wasn't the first time, and it wouldn't be the last. What set that moment apart in my life is that it was the first time I realized that I may be somewhat responsible for my actions. I knew I needed to change things, but as you can see from my list, I was looking for obstacles in my path— lack of training, lack of a mentor—but I was not looking at the primary result and resolution to my financial and lack of independence problems—me.

I'd like to say sitting there, pen in hand, a level of excitement in me as I scribbled, was the last time I had to do that or felt at a loss, but it wasn't. It wouldn't be until I did a real reality check on myself that I would begin to step out of my rut.

For this chapter, what I want to focus on is a reality check of ourselves, our tendencies, and our personalities. As you saw in the previous chapter, the first thing I did was take inventory of my life and what I wanted. In this chapter, we'll be doing the same thing, except now we will look at how we are holding ourselves back. And guess what? *Trusting people too much* is not a reality check.

Why do I start with this statement? *Trusting people too much* is not a trait that needs to be fixed. Sure, it can get you in trouble. Take, for instance, the following scenario: It's common to go to your friends and family for advice and encouragement. This is especially so when you are excited and want to share your opinions. You trust these people. Perhaps you trust them too much. Remember, family members will often try to protect one another and not always in the right way. Perhaps you are told that you are a dreamer, that you think too big, or that "nobody can ever accomplish that much success." I remember a time when I rushed over to my friend, someone I trust and respect, to share the good news. I wanted to tell him that I was going to become a public speaker. I expected him to support and cheer for me since I'd found something I was excited about. Rather, he said, "Wanny, you can't even speak correct English. Who would want to listen to you talk?" Ouch!

That story is a good example of trusting people too much, but is that a character flaw or something I need to work on? No. Trusting people is important. You will not attain any of your goals without trust. If your goal is to become a professional athlete, you need to trust your coach. If your goal is to be a successful writer, you need to trust your editor and agent. If you want to be wealthy, you need to trust your mentors. Trust is a good thing. But if you happen to be a sucker for those who are close to you and they are not someone you want to be, then I suggest you fire them.

Our goal in this chapter is to find true flaws. More importantly, our goal is find flaws that you have an ability to remedy (and most you can) and that you cannot blame others for. Imagine yourself on a deserted island. You realize you have flaws that you need to fix in order to survive. There is no one else on the island, and so there is no one to blame. Let's say you are eating too many coconuts and realize you will be out of your only food source if you don't slow down. Why do you eat too many coconuts? No self-restraint, lack of willpower, and so on.

I'll use myself as an example, and I'll start where I should have years ago. I am lazy. In fact maybe I should yell that out: *I am lazy!* There, that's my first character flaw that I need to work on. What are some others? I am impulsive, I lack self-discipline, I spend money frivolously when I have it, and I procrastinate.

Those are five examples of me. Reading those examples, you can easily see why I had no money and was living at home with my parents. Those aren't traits to be proud of, and don't think for a moment I didn't know I had those traits, even though I tried to hide from them as much as I could. Nevertheless, here I am preaching to the world, letting everyone know that not only do I have these traits but I constantly need to keep myself in check in order to not allow them back in my life. Character traits are part of your personality; they will always try to come back. The common belief is that it takes twenty-one days of consistent effort to form a new habit, while breaking one takes much longer. But the flaws I listed earlier (such as laziness and impulsiveness) are not what I would consider bad habits but rather bad traits. Traits need to be constantly monitored, or else you could easily slip back into them, regardless of how much time has passed. They are a part of you. This is why it is so important to know who you are and constantly strive to improve. Improvement puts obstacles in the regressive path to who you were and wanted to change away from.

My friend Tony once told me a story about his life and his character flaw. When Tony was in college, he got his first credit card. Soon after, he received two more, and for over a year, he didn't buy one thing. But one day, he was in a small shop and wanted a baseball card that cost $800. To me, and perhaps you, that seems a high price for a baseball card, but he really wanted it. The problem is that he didn't have money, but he did have a credit card. So he bought it. As soon as he did, he realized how easy it was to buy things on credit. Soon he had five credit cards and was $8,000 in debt. The bigger problem is that he didn't pay things back, not for years. By then, as you likely know, that debt was now much larger. It took Tony two decades to pay everything back. He lost his credit cards, and his credit scores plummeted before he even knew what a credit score was. You would think that all the problems he had were only in regard to credit cards, but they weren't. This character flaw resonated in every credit issue Tony had. He would overdraw his bank account and leave that bank and go to another until finally no bank would allow him to have an account. The same happened with rent. He seemed to never make his rent payment and was evicted time and time again. His debts kept piling up. One day, the company Tony worked for offered a financial planning seminar. Tony went, he became excited, and it really worked. He spent the next ten years focused on paying off his old debts and building a financially free life for himself.

The hardest thing for Tony to swallow was that although he always made enough money to pay off his debts, he was just too lazy to pay the bill and would sooner go out to a restaurant than pay his rent. He always assumed everything would just work out, but it rarely did. For ten years, Tony worked on paying off his debt and studying how to manage money, save money, and become more frugal. He learned the fine points of credit, credit scores, and credit monitoring. He'd always told everyone that he'd been a victim of credit card fraud and identity theft rather than put the blame on himself. He deflected it away. It was another character flaw.

After ten years, Tony paid off all his debts and knew more about how to save, manage money, work from a budget, and manage credit than nearly anyone you can imagine. He'd spent ten years obsessed with it. It had been thirty years since Tony opened that first credit card, and it took that long to pay it off. He hadn't had a credit card in over twenty years for the simple reason that the ones he had were canceled by the company, and his credit evaluations were too poor to get a new one. But, as Tony knew, if managed well, credit cards can improve your credit history. So after years of not having one, Tony applied and received a low-balance credit card. In another effort to build his credit, Tony bought CDs at a local bank and took out a secure loan on those CDs. These are both common and safe ways to build your credit.

Within two years, Tony had four credit cards all maxed out and had defaulted on his loan. The entire process started again.

So what happened? Tony had spent ten years managing everything without an issue and had in fact repaired problems of his previous twenty years. How could it happen again with his discipline, new habits, and knowledge? It's simple. Once Tony had credit available to him again, he assumed his troubles were over and let his guard down. He no longer felt that he had to focus on credit and money management. He felt as if it would all come naturally because he had broken his bad habits. But he didn't break his character traits, those inner demons sitting inside him, looking to break out. If Tony had said to himself, *Okay, I now have credit; I have a chance to not just catch up but also improve myself, and as long as I maintain my discipline, I will be fine*, he wouldn't have been just fine; he would have been extremely successful. In those ten years, Tony had paid off more than $100,000 in debt. Within five years of that, he'd accumulated more than $15,000 of additional debt by letting his guard down.

In our exercise on creating a reality check for yourself, I want you to keep in mind these two principles:

1. Poor character traits are traits you alone can change—no one else. When looking for them, pretend you are on a deserted island and you are the only one responsible for yourself.

2. For practical purposes, habits are formed in twenty-one days. Good habits can be broken much sooner. Negative personality traits and character

flaws, if not constantly managed, can always return, regardless of time.

For your exercise, I want you to think of at least five character flaws that may be holding you back in life or that you are interested in changing. Remember the key points above. For me, I have listed these flaws:

1. I am lazy.

2. I am impulsive.

3. I lack self-discipline.

4. When I have it, I spend money frivolously.

5. I procrastinate.

Look at your notes from the previous chapter and break down your problems. The root cause of your problems is likely your character flaws. For example, let's assume you make $50,000 a year. Congratulations—you make more than about 95 percent of the world. As a single person, you should easily be able to live off that income, right? Well, you're not. You are in Tony's position. So what could be the root cause of those problems? Lack of organization? Procrastination? Laziness? Inability to manage money? Misunderstanding of money? The traits are numerous, but for you, what are they?

You are reading my book for a reason. But what is that reason? Are any of the following statements true for you?

• Have a problem holding a job?

- Find yourself late on every occasion?

- Have no money?

- Find yourself in debt?

- Not know your direction in life?

- Have trouble maintaining a relationship?

- Have trouble finding friends or meeting new people?

- Find yourself stuck in a job you hate?

- Have credit problems?

- Have anger management problems?

- Have addiction problems?

These are all character flaws to some degree, and some worse than others, but none are impossible to find a way out of. It takes time, effort, and a frequent reality check on your behaviors and how to manage them.

I don't want you to feel frustrated, overwhelmed, or upset with yourself. Remember that everyone has negative traits, even successful people. But the first step in fixing those traits is to know or acknowledge them. I hope that you can see the benefit in coming out and saying, "This is me now, and this is what I want to change."

Identifying our flaws can be difficult. Think about a job interview. You are trying to make yourself look good to a potential employer. But then they say, "Tell me some of your character flaws." Well, we all have answers for this, right? We all care too much, we try too hard, and we are overly dedicated. But what is it that your potential employer is looking for? They want to know if you can acknowledge that you are not perfect. Not only that, they want to know if you know your negative traits and what you do to manage them. A smart employer recognizes that everyone has bad traits; everyone has different traits, but those people all need to find a way to manage those traits and work together.

Unlike the answers most give to that interview question, be real with yourself, and take this seemingly easy task seriously.

If you cannot think of negative traits, or if you are having difficulty prioritizing or determining if a trait is negative or not, here are a few exercises to help you along:

Reach out to others.

Reach out to people you trust and are comfortable with. Explain to them that you are having problems, although how much you explain is up to you. Tell them you are trying to improve yourself and that you are purposefully looking for less-than-positive traits. You can approach friends, parents, colleagues, a leader, your significant other, children, or anyone else you are comfortable talking to.

List specific situations.

Another way of identifying your negative traits is to make a list of specific situations that made you uncomfortable or unhappy. What was your role in that situation? How did you feel? Maybe your credit card was declined. Maybe you yelled at someone and had to apologize. What character flaws led to that situation?

List your parents' flaws.

This may seem simple to many, but list your parents' character flaws and negative traits. Why is this important? By understanding our background, we understand ourselves. Often, as people age, they realize how similar to their parents they actually are. Your personality is in your experiences, and your parents have influenced many of your experiences.

I had a friend who once told me that he looks at his parents as a tool for his life. He tries to emulate their positive traits and improve on or resist the negative ones, because he knows he inherited all of them to some degree. I always thought that was a great example of improving yourself.

Write your version of the flaw.

Once you have identified possible character flaws, choose one of them, and write your version of the flaw. Be hard on yourself. Tell the truth, and be blunt. How do you think you look to others when you are performing that trait? If you are perpetually late, how do you think that makes someone feel who depends on you to be on time? Don't look at it from how others react to you being late but rather how important it was that you were on time and what the consequences a person had for you being late were.

How does your flaw affect others?

Look at how this trait affects those around you. How are people in your life affected by your actions? Are they affected emotionally or physically? Or are they always lending you money they know they will never see again? Does that make you proud? Do you disappoint your parents or children? Knowing the impact of your traits is important in understanding the need to improve.

Identifying traits to improve on is not necessarily a five-minute exercise, and I would suggest taking time with it, even if it takes you a week. Many of us have spent time developing these flaws to work for us. It will take time to understand our flaws and how to improve on them. For some of us, it will take time to understand that we have character flaws like everyone else. If you want to know how much the character flaw has taken over your life, then take a week or two to track your trait. Every time you find yourself using a specific trait, note the situation, what occurred, what the outcome or consequence was, and how it affected you and others. You don't need to try to repair the flaw during these two weeks, but you should be aware of it. It is similar to logging your food and daily calories. Awareness is the start of changing a behavior.

Once you feel you have found the traits you want to improve on, you should feel a sense of accomplishment. In many cases, you will feel as if you are further in reaching your goals than you have ever been before.

I know, for me, sitting down and identifying what I wanted in life, my goals, and my obstacles gave me a huge sense of relief. I felt I was on my way to success. However, it wasn't until I discovered my own flaws were holding me back and identified them that I felt that weight on my back finally begin to fall away. This is the moment I knew I would accomplish my goals, rather than just knowing what my goals were.

Chapter 3 Review and Lesson Plan

In chapter 3, we discussed personal flaws that have either contributed to where we are in life and that we want to change or flaws that make it difficult for us to overcome. It is okay to have a personal flaw. We all have them. What is important to remember is that you do not have to go through life with your flaws always in tow. You have the ability to change and improve. In this chapter, I have given you numerous ways of answering a question, which on paper seems easy to do, but when you try to do it, it may be difficult.

The activity for this chapter is to write five character flaws that contribute to the difficulties you are having—or may have—in achieving your goal. Do your homework if you can't figure out five. Elicit the help of friends and family, even if it may be a difficult conversation to have or to hear from the mouths of others. Remember, you are trying to accomplish something, and you must be honest with yourself in doing so.

CHAPTER 4

Game Plan

In every aspect of life, have a game plan, and then do your best to achieve it.

—Alan Kulwicki

If you've been following the exercises outlined in previous chapters, you will find you have goals for what you want to attain and the personal obstacles in your path. These personal obstacles are traits and characteristics you have that we could consider negative flaws. Remember, everyone has flaws, but the successful are the ones who identify, acknowledge, and manage them. The goal in this chapter is to try to develop a game plan—something you can tangibly hold and work off.

Achieving your goals requires proper planning. Now that we have identified what is holding you back, we can now look at defining your purpose. What is it that you want out of life? Do you want money, emotional stability, a successful relationship, happiness? Why do you want it? Security, flexibility, or to feel loved? There are many answers to both of these questions, and I've likely not listed yours, so like all other exercises and questions, take your time to think about what you want and are looking for. Remember, your objective is to reach your goal, and goals are typically long and consistent routes to success. So, be patient with yourself, think, focus, and prepare yourself for success.

Whatever your purpose, big or small, write it down.

You may have heard the saying, "Money does not make you happy. Some would rather be poor and happy than be rich and miserable." Whether this pertains to you is something you need to figure out. I have had friends who had few objects of value, yet were very happy. I have been on both sides, poor and wealthy. While I can understand someone who is poor being happy, I'd rather be wealthy. Wealth provides me with the freedom of time—freedom to spend time with family and friends, freedom to do the things which matter most in my life, such as public speaking, writing, and traveling. Wealth offers me the opportunity to put aside my past worries of paying the bills, worrying if I will have a place to live tomorrow or food to feed my family. Those are obstacles that take time if I don't have the money to simply pay them off. Money is not my only goal, but I realize—like many immigrants who came from poverty—that money does not make me happy but certainly allows freedom to not worry as much about life.

In addition to the freedom money allows, it is also important to me to be on a proper spiritual path. I want my mind in harmony with my body. Spirituality and harmony are a gateway to developing focus and the ability to think clearly. Through prayer and meditation, you can harness your thoughts and concentrate on not only your future goals but also managing your negative flaws. Spirituality can mentally prepare you to be open to new ideas and help you maintain a positive mental attitude.

To live a balanced life, you need to have good health, happiness, fulfilling relationships, a sense of well-being, creative freedom, and, most of all, the enjoyment of life. You are not living life if you do not enjoy what you are doing.

In many of my speaking engagements, I talk about finding your passion, *a strong and barely controllable emotion.* Have you ever felt so passionate about something you can barely control yourself? I see it watching tennis on television. These players are so motivated by what they are doing that when they hit a winner, they scream out, jump, pump their fists, and sometimes emotionally break down into tears. It can be overwhelming just to watch, but to experience, even more so. It is amazing the emotions passion can draw out. Once you feel it filling your body and pumping blood through coursing veins, you'll never want to forget the feeling. I truly believe passion is the spark that ignites the fire. Without passion, there is no action. Once you find your passion, you will wake up every morning full of hope and ready to tackle any challenges that lie in your path.

The first step to your goal—your passion—is to have a game plan. For many people, losing weight is a multiyear or decades-long struggle. Obesity is considered a plague across America. With that comes an increase in fad diets. These diets will promise you quick progress in a short time with minimal effort. But are they sustainable? Usually not. Often, people will be drawn into quick weight loss, and they do in fact lose twenty pounds or more quickly. But what happens in a year? In most cases, those people gain that weight back. They do this because they have found a technique that helps them reach their goal—a gimmick or even a scheme—but they do not have a game plan. They are not teaching themselves how to lose weight effectively and keep that weight off. In their minds, they are too busy to focus on losing weight and all the other things that come with life. They think, *I want to lose the weight now and never have to worry about it again.* Well, guess what? If you go into anything impulsively, you will get out of it what you put into it.

Developing a game plan for your life is much like crafting or molding a new life. You must take control and an active role in shaping your future. You are the only person who has the ability to control every facet of your life. Think of your game plan as your life's blueprint.

Creating Your Blueprint

Are you living the life you want to have, or are you going through the motions in order to feel as though you are appeasing others, or trying to be a part of what society demands? Remember when I told you how my parents wanted me to be successful? I thought they meant I should be a doctor or lawyer, but when I was at my lowest point, my mother took me aside. She told me it wasn't those occupations she wanted; it was my happiness. Her words resonate with me often. While I tried to achieve those objectives and failed miserably, I forgot one important detail. I never had a plan. I just figured things would all fall into place.

Being a mature adult means knowing where you're going in life and having a plan, especially for something as important as life.

Unfortunately, many people today just drift along and let life happen to them. Maybe you're one of them. I know I've spent much of my life drifting and wandering, letting life happen to me rather than taking control of it. It is a sense of helplessness, and the sooner you allow this to happen, the more helpless you will become.

Have you ever experienced the helpless, anxious feeling that you don't have control of your life and your future, and you have no idea what to do about it?

Well, today is the day you are going to do something about it. You are going to take your lists of what you want and your personal obstacles, and you are going to put together a game plan to change your life—not just for now or a year from now but for life. As they say, *Give a man a fish, and he eats for a day. Teach a man to fish, and he eats his whole life.* Well, you are about to teach yourself to fish.

When I sat down and started writing my first e-book, *The Five Laws to Wealth, Success, and Happiness*, I thought that everything I wrote had to be unique. But as I began to write, I realized that I was often referring to those mentors I'd originally read about. I quoted Zig Ziglar, took ideas from Thomas Jefferson, and pondered ideas from Steve Jobs. These were successful people I admired and wanted to emulate. I remember reading something once (although the writer's name escapes me) that there are no new ideas, only new perspectives. The writer spoke about how growing up he was influenced by Stephen King, Lloyd Alexander, and F. Scott Fitzgerald. If you were to take those three men, spin them around in a pot, and then pour out the contents, you would be pouring out his writing style. You see, he wasn't any of those men, and he did not write like them, but he did take bits and pieces of each to form his own style. I've applied this same principle to the steps below, and I strongly suggest you do so, as well. Every one of us is different in our experiences. Emulating what worked for one person may not work for you, but taking pieces from many people will help you find that blueprint for your life. So before we start with the steps I have below, please take time to make a list of traits and game plans others have taken, and see if you think any of those will help you along your journey. Remember, my book (as well as others) is merely a guide of what has worked for me. It is an inspirational journey to show you how I did it. It is an inspirational guide to help you achieve your goals and step out of your rut. It is a way to show you steps to define who you are, define what you want, and set you on the path of self-discovery, which in turn leads to fulfilling your life goal or overcoming obstacles you currently face.

Building your blueprint is a mix of Stephen Covey's *7 Habits of Highly Effective People*, Richard Carlson's *Don't Sweat the Small Stuff*, and a variety of experiences and books I've come across over the years.

Where Do You Build Your Blueprint?

I've mentioned this a few times already, but it should be mentioned again: developing a life game plan is a large project and as such will require patience and time. This is not a quick resolution to solving your problems and moving forward. I will be asking you to do a lot of thinking, note taking, list making, and evaluation of who you are. You may be surprised to find out how difficult—and at times draining—this is. You are being asked to dig deep within yourself and do something many people have difficulty with—be honest with yourself. Often, obstacles come from hiding from yourself and your own traits. Outside obstacles may not exist at all.

After you have completed the steps in the first three chapters (your evaluations), I suspect it will take you anywhere from a weekend to a full week of commitment to put together your blueprint. In terms of hours, you could take twenty hours depending on your personal research and goals. It helps if you can disappear from life for a weekend. Head to a cabin in the woods, a hotel in a city you've never been to, or a bed-and-breakfast in a quaint river town. This is a journey of exploration and of growth. You should be in a place that is inspirational and comfortable for you, a place that will help you realize what you are looking for and inspire you to get there. Obviously, this is not something everyone can afford to do. Well, there are places near all of us to get away that aren't costly. Try a new coffee shop, a park, or the beach, or (if it suits you) sit on a pile of clothes in a large closet. The point is that you need to hide away from your everyday distractions. Remember the quote about insanity? If you do the same thing over and over again, you cannot expect a different outcome.

How Do You Display Your Blueprint?

All of us work differently. For example, some writers edit their own work on the computer, while others need to print out each page and use a pen or pencil. If you're a techy type of person, maybe it would be better to use a Word document or even a spreadsheet. Maybe you work better with a one-dollar notebook, or perhaps you want a fancy leather-bound folder and notepad. Many people think they feel more invested with a pen and paper rather than a keyboard. Others feel a digital program helps them think and organize more clearly. There are positives to both. The important thing is that you take the time to write down your game plan. You'll need it in the future.

Defining Who You Are

Every one of us throughout life will play multiple roles, and in those roles, we will act differently at different stages of our lives. Our roles last for years and decades but are sometimes as short as a day. Long-term roles, such as spouse, parent, and friend, take years to develop and grow into, and they are often ever evolving. Short-term roles, such as leader for a daylong project or carpool driver, are swift and often dependent on previous life experiences. We each, during the course of our lives, will hold several dozen to hundreds and possibly thousands of roles. This can be overwhelming. Similar to the expression "jack-of-all-trades, master of none," we need to evaluate our goals to determine where we can excel. Hopefully, by the end of this short exercise, we can knock off some of these roles in our lives that we perform unnecessarily. This exercise is not to find what you can take away but rather it should help you define your current roles in life so you can focus on the ones most important to you and become master of some of your trades, instead of jack-of-all.

What I would like you to do is to grab your pen and paper or computer and start jotting down the roles you take on every day. Similar to brainstorming, write down everything that comes to mind. I'll start you off with a few of my own:

- husband

- son

- brother

- uncle

- friend

- public speaker

- writer

- mentor

- leader

- citizen

- student

- entrepreneur

It's interesting that we spend so much of our time stressing over simple events in our lives, yet we don't spend the time developing and growing those roles that are important to us.

I'll give you an example of a friend of mine. He works for a large health club chain. He loves his job, has a good position, and does well. Yet he is passionate about writing, and he's good at it. Ever since he was young, all he could think about was writing. He would like to one day work from home as a full-time writer. However, when he gets home from working all day, he is given a choice: Do I sit down and write, or do I hang out with friends? I bet you can figure out what option I'm going to tell you he takes, and you're right. He chooses hanging out with his friends. Consequently, my friend is in his late forties and has spent his entire life dreaming of being a writer, wondering why he never had the opportunity to become one. If he stays the course, he will never achieve the goal that, for him, seemed to be a lifelong dream. Because he has not pursued the dream beyond an occasional couple of weeks of writing per year, I have seen him slowly fall into resentment toward anyone who is successful (at any level) in writing. He has also become, to a degree, depressed; instead of going out with friends, he will sit at home contemplating what he did wrong to not become a writer, all the while . . . not writing.

I imagine my parents' roles when they chose to leave Vietnam.

- parent

- immigrant

- risk-taker

- adventurer

- role model

- spouse

While some of their goals are the same, I have to think that their route in life affected them much more deeply than mine did. My siblings and I didn't have much growing up in my years after starting school, but my parents had much less.

While I had to follow my parents out of Vietnam, my parents had to shoulder the responsibility of their children. They had to forgo their own concerns about themselves and focus on those around them. They may not have written down their roles, but they certainly knew them and were forced to prioritize them for the sake of keeping their family alive.

In order to guide us through our long-term goals, we need to write down our roles, prioritize them, and decide what is important to us. So take your list and start writing a number next to each role, from most important to least important.

What you'll likely see is that you have a crazy number of roles you take on. This isn't surprising. We, as humans, tend to take on tasks, roles, and goals, yet we rarely realize the importance of dropping things from our lives. Take me, for example. I want to be a writer, mentor, public speaker, real estate broker, and so on. How can I possibly excel at any of those if I take them all on? The answer is that I will need to drop something. The same is true of your list. As you go through it, evaluate your roles. Is one causing you more stress than another? Are there roles in your life that do not fulfill you or give you anything, whether emotionally, physically, or monetarily? Do you have roles that take away from other roles without giving back? If you find these roles in your life, you may want to consider trimming them from your list. It will be difficult. We are not programmed to trim away something we've taken on, but in order for you to succeed at your goals and priorities in life, it is sometimes necessary to drop a few things holding you back.

Once you have your prioritized list completed, you will likely find, as with many of the previous exercises, that a little more weight has been lifted from your shoulders. Hopefully, you can start seeing some of the progress toward achieving the goals you desire. With your prioritized list of roles, you can now start leading your choices in a direction more suitable to what your goals in life are. This list will be helpful when you need to make decisions in life that may take away from what you value or when you make decisions that might have a negative impact on your goals.

Take, for example, a job offer with a higher salary that required you to travel extensively, perhaps being out of town four to five days a week. This job will financially benefit your family, but you will also lose out on being with your family. Now if you listed father and spouse above employee, then your list would be a good indicator that making this career change would negatively impact your future goals and what you cherish in life.

Remember that this list is not permanent. You will take on new roles, you will lose others, and your priorities will change. Take that same scenario I just mentioned and put yourself fifteen years in the future when your kids are grown and out on their own. Maybe your spouse has a good family core where you live, and it is not important for you to be home all the time. In that case, it may be more beneficial for you to take that career change.

Define Your Purpose for Each Role

Now that you know your roles in life, it is important to define your purpose for each role. Without a sense of purpose, you wander without meaning, and you cannot hope to master your role or ultimately master the goals you want in life.

What I'm going to ask you to do next is to write your own eulogy. Morbid, right? Darn right it is, but by picturing the end, you will know better how to get to the end. In the movie *Serendipity*, Dean Kansky is trying to convince his friend Jonathan Trager to not give up in his search for his soul mate. As a writer, Dean Kansky realizes the effect a eulogy can have on someone. Whether it is in reflection or regret, a eulogy is a summary of life and achievements and, in some cases, failures. Take a look at the eulogy Dean Kansky wrote for his still-living friend:

> *Jonathan Trager, prominent television producer for ESPN, died last night from complications of losing his soul mate and his fiancée. He was thirty-five years old. Soft-spoken and obsessive, Trager never looked the part of a hopeless romantic. But in the final days of his life, he revealed an unknown side of his psyche. This hidden, quasi-Jungian persona surfaced during the Agatha Christie–like pursuit of his long reputed soul mate, a woman whom he only spent a few precious hours with. Sadly, the protracted search ended late Saturday night in complete and utter failure. Yet even in certain defeat, the courageous Trager secretly clung to the belief that life is not merely a series of meaningless accidents or coincidences. Uh-uh. But rather, it's a tapestry of events that culminate in an exquisite, sublime plan. Asked about the loss of his dear friend, Dean Kansky, the Pulitzer Prize–winning author and executive editor of the* New York Times, *described Jonathan as a changed man in the last days of his life. "Things were clearer for him," Kansky noted. Ultimately, Jonathan*

concluded that if we are to live life in harmony with the universe, we must all possess a powerful faith in what the ancients used to call "fatum," what we currently refer to as destiny.

Now let's pretend for a moment that you are Jonathan Trager, and your friend read you this eulogy while you were still alive. What would you do? Would you give up, as Jonathan did in this scene, or would you realize the regrets you would harbor if you did not seek out your goal?

Think of your life now and your life when you die. Imagine your friends, family, and coworkers at your funeral. Now imagine what they would say about you. What would be the highlights of your life? Now imagine your life if you had achieved your goals. Do you see a difference?

Define Goals for Yourself

Now that you know your roles, let's go back and look at how to attain your goals. Everyone reading this book is doing so because they are trying to find a way to achieve their goals and become successful. These goals can vary from losing weight to becoming wealthy. What is most important is that you are setting a goal and making sure that this goal is yours, not one you think someone else wants you to have.

For many years, I wasted my time focusing on goals that didn't suit me. In high school, my parents gave me four career choices to choose from: doctor, lawyer, accountant, or engineer. I didn't want to disappoint them, so I had to choose one of the four. First, I was terrible in math, so that alone eliminated two out of the four choices, engineering and accounting. As a shy and quiet guy, would you want me to represent you in court? I didn't think so. Lawyer, too, was out the door. The only thing left was for me to become a doctor. Let's see, "Dr. Huynh." I like the sound of that. Off to college I went to become Dr. Huynh. To make a long story short, after two years in college, I realized becoming a doctor wasn't something I wanted to do. So I did what many billionaires did: I dropped out of school. I'm sharing this with you because, rather than chasing what I wanted to do, I was chasing the dream my parents planned for me. Only when I was at my lowest point in my life and had a heart-to-heart talk with my parents did they give me their blessing to chase my own dream. Once they gave me their blessing, I felt a weight lifted from my shoulders. I was free to pursue whatever dream my heart desired. Discover what it is that excites you, and then go after it wholeheartedly. Only then will you be able to live a fulfilling life.

Rule number one of goal setting is to make these goals yours. You should not set goals because you think that's what you should be doing. You set goals because those are the goals you want to have.

Some people know what their goals are and without a thought can tell you. "I want to lose one hundred pounds." "I want to have $5 million in the bank so I can stay at home and start my own business." But for those of you who have goals but don't yet know which one you should tackle, make a list. Yeah, I know . . . another list. Jot down every goal you can think of, whether it's regarding health, career, finances, travel, spirituality—everything. Write down as many as you can think of.

Now that you have that big list, narrow it down to five goals with the mind-set that these are the goals you want to work on over the next five years. Common goals are paying off all debt, writing a book, traveling to Italy, losing weight. I'm going use a cliché for a moment here, but remember, "Vague goals produce vague results." You will hear this saying over and again at any goal setting or self-help seminar, and it's true. So let's put some detail behind your goals. Turn them into something specific and attainable.

I will lose one hundred pounds by January 20, 20XX.

I will finish writing my first novel by June 10, 20XX.

I will complete my first marathon at the Twin Cities Marathon in 20XX.

Now that you know your roles in life and have set five attainable goals to focus on for the next five years, you have likely started the next phase of our process: visualization.

Chapter 4 Review and Lesson Plan

Chapter 4 is all about building a blueprint of your current life and what you would like your life to be like, basing the blueprint off the roles you take on. Everyone plays multiple roles in their lives.

Exercise 1 is to brainstorm and identify as many roles as you can that you hold. These can be parent, sibling, friend, citizen—any role you can think of. Regardless of how small you think that role is, I want you to write it down.

Exercise 2 is to prioritize your goals by writing a number next to each one. The role most important to you would be a one, while the least important would be the last on your list.

Now that you have your roles defined, you can start putting together goals that fit into your roles. Most of us know what we want in life, but without identifying who we are and why we want that goal, it can be difficult to achieve what we are looking for. This chapter is about defining who you are. Later in the book, I will discuss how to put together a goal-setting game plan to push you through to success.

CHAPTER 5

Visualization

Visualize this thing that you want, see it, feel it, believe in it. Make your mental blueprint, and begin to build.

—Robert Collier

Many of the greatest men and women accomplish big, seemingly impossible things because they can visualize the future. They have developed the ability to conceptualize themselves in the future and see themselves doing great things. The art of visualization is not a new concept; for some, it seems to be a natural ability, yet others—myself included—need to train their minds to think this way.

I unknowingly began using this technique when I was eight years old. Our family was living in the detention camp in Thailand; there was a bus station outside the camp. Once a day, the bus came and took one or two lucky families off to America. Every day, I sat and watched as those lucky families boarded the bus to freedom. I saw the joy and excitement on their faces as they stepped on the bus. In their minds, they were already free. What lay ahead for them was unknown, but they did know they were free from the strife they found in their homeland. In their minds, they were free from worry, free from poverty, free from struggling, and free from starvation. I kept telling myself that one day it was going to be my family's turn.

Every day at the bus station, I would sit long after the bus had pulled away and was out of sight and all the well-wishers had left. I sat and let my mind dream of the life I would be enjoying once I was in America. I pictured my family boarding the bus and the joy I would feel once I stepped inside. It didn't happen overnight or the week after, but I didn't stop visualizing my family boarding that bus.

Sometimes we have to act like little kids and just dream, play make-believe in our minds. Now, so many years later, I understand why I went to the bus station every day. I went there so I could feel the power of visualization. Everything I felt and saw was so vivid and strong. Even today I can remember my emotions, and I fully believed it was going to happen. We *were* going to go to get on that bus.

Sure enough, one day, my dad rushed home to give us the good news. "We're going to America!"

The excitement, the joy—everything was so overwhelming. There were many sleepless nights of anticipation. Our family's dream was going to become a reality.

Once we arrived in America, I got caught up in the challenges and opportunities our new home offered. I slowly lost touch with the feeling I had sitting at that bus stop. It wasn't until I started studying those who had made it, the great and successful people who inspire me, that I recalled my childhood experience with visualization.

Once I remembered how powerful visualization could be, I began to incorporate it into my daily adult life. At one point, when I didn't have any money, I was intent on buying my dream car. I went to the dealer to test-drive the car. I sat inside, wrapped my hands around the steering wheel, and pictured myself owning it one day.

A year and a half later, I was driving that car.

I began to apply this technique to every area of my life. I visualized the house I wanted to live in and the places where I wanted to travel. Over time, I was able to accomplish my goals and began to live the life I had created for myself. The things I have visualized are now becoming real for me.

I wish for all that and more to happen to you! Without visualization, there is no motivation to push for your dreams. As Einstein once said, "Imagination is more important than knowledge." How true is that! You don't have to be the smartest or the brightest kid to be successful. All you need is the ability to use your mind. It doesn't take much labor to do it. We can all accomplish great things once we put our brains to work.

Realize that God has given you the world's most powerful asset—your mind. Take a look around. Many of the biggest advancements we take for granted today would never have existed if it weren't for those who dared to dream. Few thought the Wright Brothers would actually succeed in their endeavors to make a flying machine. Yet they and their team pushed through all the setbacks and roadblocks and surprised the world with their success. Because of people like them and countless others, we as a society benefit.

The next great thing could be *your* idea.

One of my dreams was to become a professional speaker.

I didn't know where or how to start this, but the dream was always in my mind. The seed was planted fifteen years ago when I got a call from one of my high school classmates. I had just dropped out of college. The phone rang, and I picked it up to hear a familiar voice on the other end of the line. He seemed excited. I don't know if he was happy to hear my voice or if he was on drugs of some kind. I told him I was in the middle of something, and I couldn't talk. Little did he know he was interrupting my episode of *Gilligan's Island*. He insisted that I give him a few minutes that could change my life. Okay, he got my attention, and since *Gilligan's Island* was on commercial, I let him continue. He insisted I get out of my underwear and go with him to a motivational seminar. First, how did he know I was in my undies? Second, how did he know I didn't have anything else better to do with my time? My choice was clear. I could either stay home in my boxers and watch the rerun of *Gilligan's Island* or go out and be amused by some guy who I knew nothing of.

Before he hung up, he said, "Wanny, this guy will change your life."

Next thing I knew, I found myself in a room of three hundred strangers. I took a seat next to my buddy, who was still smiling from ear to ear as we waited for the speaker to be introduced. I surveyed the crowd. It was a mixed crowd, young and old, mostly men. I began to feel out of place, being that we were the only two Asians in the room. As the speaker was introduced, everyone jumped on to their feet and began cheering and clapping. I didn't want to be the only oddball in the room sitting there with my arms crossed, so I got up on my feet and joined in. The energy in the room was overwhelming.

I took my seat before the clapping died down. This was my first time in a live seminar, and I didn't know what to expect. Prior to this, the closest I'd gotten to a motivational speaker was hearing Tony Robbins's tape in one of my friend's cars. I must admit the speaker did a great job of maintaining my attention span. Normally, my mind tends to drift off to la-la land within a few short minutes of conversation. I think I was able to pay attention longer because I viewed him as a successful businessman, someone I wanted to be. At that time, I considered anyone who was wearing a three-piece suit to be an international businessman.

Midway through his speech, he said something that was so moving and inspiring it sent chills up my spine. Next thing I knew, I had goose bumps all over my body. I felt the hairs rising at the back of my neck. I began to sit up straight in my chair and focus my attention on the speaker.

I wish I still remembered who the speaker was. At that moment, he awoke the sleeping giant. I told myself that I wanted to do that. I want to move people the way he moved me. Most of all, I want to give people goose bumps.

After his speech, I remember feeling, *Wow, that was so moving, so inspiring.* I pictured myself on stage sharing my stories. Who would have thought my friend was right? The speaker did change my life.

I knew I wanted to become a speaker, but I didn't know how or where to begin. My dream of motivating and inspiring people was pushed aside as I began to chase other dreams and passions.

Then one day, a coworker of mine said, "Wanny, your life is such an interesting story. Why not write a book?"

Who would want to read a book about me? I thought. *I'm a nobody.* Before I could write about my life, I reasoned, I needed to have something to prove to the world. I needed to be successful; otherwise, who would want to listen to a guy like me? So what did I end up doing? I went out in search of success. Thus, I shot myself down before I even started writing, and in the pursuit of success, I ended up taking my eyes off the big picture—doing what I love and following my passion.

I didn't begin to take action on my dream of becoming a speaker until I was in my midthirties when I came across *The Success Principles* by Jack Canfield. In one of the chapters, it felt as if Jack was addressing me directly. He said, "Wanny, if you want to become a speaker, join Toastmasters and start speaking." The light went on in my head. *That's it? All I need to do is join Toastmasters, and I can start speaking?*

I say it here as if it were so simple. *Oh! Toastmasters! Problem solved.* But, in what you have read so far, has it ever been that easy? No, of course not. In addition, with me and all my personal obstacles, I knew it would be difficult still. Toastmasters did not solve all my problems, but what it did do was help me harness my potential and show me what I was capable of doing.

As I'd said earlier, despite unknowingly using visualization as a child, I had to reteach myself what it was to visualize my future. For people down on their luck and looking to pull themselves out of a hole, this can oftentimes be difficult.

What I didn't realize as a child is that while I watched those buses come and go each day, my parents had been visualizing our arrival in America much longer than I had ever known. It would be silly for me to think as an eight-year-old I was able to save my family by visualizing our trip to America. But it would not be silly to say both of my parents visualized and acted upon their intentions. They are the reason my family survived the trip and finally made it to Minnesota. They were the ones who saw the future and their dreams. They were the ones who harnessed the power of visualization.

I have a friend who once told me that as a teenager growing up, he dreamed of beating Pete Sampras in a tennis match. To him, it was reality. He never once thought he did not have the ability. He says that now, in his midthirties, he realizes he would have never won that match. It wouldn't have been possible. However, as a kid, he could see every shot he would make; he could feel the sweat on his body and the ache in his legs. He could see himself doing that. While maybe he would not have beaten Pete Sampras, he would use that thought process, the visualization of playing Pete Sampras, to become a competitive and successful collegiate tennis player. He didn't have the coaches, money, or even the greatest racquet, but he did have a focus and ability to see himself as a great player, playing a great player.

Mental imagery is something athletes have been utilizing for decades to boost their strength, confidence, and overall performance. The technique can be used for more than just sports. Everyone can use mental imagery to perform well. My friend the tennis player recalls the first time he realized what mental imagery was:

It was part of an experiment in my eighth-grade class. The teacher took five students; I was one of them. They also took five of our best basketball players. For one week, we all practiced shooting free throws together. The second week, the non–basketball players were separated from the basketball players. While the kids who played on the team continued to practice shooting free throws every day for an hour, the group I was in was brought to a room. We would lie down on the floor, and a psychologist would come in and tell us to close our eyes. Then she would take us through shooting a free throw. She would do this over and over, each time changing the shot just a little, but every time we would make the shot. At the end of our imagery session, we would each take ten shots on the court. After a week of this, we had a school-wide free-throw shooting competition between the five imagery students and the basketball team. The non–basketball players won 42–35.

This is a great example of what studies have found over the years. Visualization along with performance training often does better than simply physical practice. It is the art of visualization.

The Basics

"Imagery can't make you perform beyond your capabilities, but it can help you reach your potential," says Tom Seabourne, an athlete and imagery expert and the author of *The Complete Idiot's Guide to Quick Total Body Workouts*. So I want to be clear: visualization is a tool to get you where you want to be; it is not a save-all for your life. I would hate for someone to imagine being a millionaire, tossing money left and right, and months later not being anywhere near his or her goal. But visualization does help you see yourself as you have not seen yourself before. Think of it as a walk in the country at night. You are just walking. Your goal may be out there somewhere, but without having a road or lights, you will have a heck of a time finding it, although you may happen upon it by accident. But put in the lights (visualization) and a paved road (your tools) and you easily find your way to your goal.

Use All Your Senses

The most effective imagery involves all five senses. My friend who played tennis said that he could feel the tingle of sweat dripping down his back and the smell of a freshly opened can of tennis balls when he visualized playing Pete Sampras. Try to use all your senses when you are imagining how you will get to your goal. If your goal is running a marathon, visualize tasting the saltiness of your sweat on your lips and the burning of the sun on your arms. You can feel a cool breeze hit you as you turn a corner and the pain in the arches of your feet.

If your goal is to lose weight, imagine sliding your hand along a thin waistline, or the ability to run up stairs without being short of breath. It's important to try to use all your senses. Close your eyes and think of them one by one. Sight, hearing, taste, touch, and smell.

First-Person Imagery

You've heard the term in writing classes. *First person* is you telling a story that happened to you. It is the same thing with imagery. You are not looking at yourself; you are acting out the practice. As in the free throws, it is important that you see yourself taking the shot, as if you were actually taking the shot. Don't visualize yourself from a distance. Be there; be in the shot.

Practice

I recently read a passage in the magazine *Real Simple*: "Effective mental imagery is not wishful thinking, nor is it brief moments of 'seeing' success," says Michael Gervais, Ph.D., a performance psychologist in Los Angeles. You can't become a better speaker simply by reading a book on the subject. "The only way we get better at mental imagery is by practicing it," says Tammy Miller, a speech coach in State College, Pennsylvania, and a speaker for Toastmasters International.

The imagery should be so real that imagining the activity should take just as long as it would take in real life. For example, if I am giving a speech, I will practice over and over until I have it down. I will physically do it in front of a mirror or friends. I will also lie down in bed, close my eyes, and picture myself on the stage in front of the actual audience. So when I am giving my speech, it is as if I have given it a dozen times already.

Give Yourself a Challenge

Challenges are an interesting way to visualize what you are doing. For example, when I am visualizing myself on stage, it helps if I can identify a few areas where a heckler may chime in. What would I say? What would I do? Well, I've never had a heckler before, but after practicing, I can confidently say I am well prepared.

Visualization can be used in any goal-setting activity. A successful career can be visualized as you on a Bluetooth device in your penthouse New York office closing a deal. What do you see outside from thirty stories up? What are you sipping on? Hot green tea? Cold coffee? Are the floors wood, and do your shoes making a tapping sound every time you step? Does your office smell of fine leather?

If you want to lose weight, visualize yourself with good eating habits. Imagine reaching for an apple on the counter, taking it in your hands. Imagine the smell of it when you take that first bite and tiny sprays of juice tickle the tip of your nose. Visualize yourself completing good habits in order to break the bad ones.

Chapter 5 Review and Lesson Plan

In chapter 5, I talk about visualization. Up to this point, we have looked at who you are and what you want to become. Visualization is a technique of building your mind-set to believe you are what you want to become. Whether you are battling cancer or striving to pull yourself out of debt, visualization can help you focus on your target.

The only exercise in this chapter is to visualize, or meditate, on your goal. Using your five senses, try to see yourself after you have obtained your goal. If your goal is to lose weight, then visualize sliding your hand along a smooth waist or getting dressed in front of a mirror and having a beautiful body.

The more you can see yourself as who you want to become, the easier it will be to get there.

CHAPTER 6

Path of Least Resistance

Courage is resistance to fear, mastery of fear,
not absence of fear.

—Mark Twain

One of the built-in truths of nature is that all elements—from tiny subparticles to animals, people, and even well-designed machines—will naturally choose the path of least resistance or effort. We can use this guiding principle to our advantage, learning how to accomplish more by doing less and learning how to overcome the illusory obstacles in our way.

Many of us *know* what needs to be done in order to be successful, but we prevent ourselves from taking those steps due to fear and uncertainty. I am guilty of this myself; I delayed many opportunities out of fear. Once I learned how to recognize and remove fear from my life, the path became much easier and natural, just like water that naturally flows downstream.

The secret is taking that first step, to act as if you cannot fail, even if you feel like you will. The hardest step is always that first step.

Relating back to my childhood and the story of how my brother and I were captured, it is obvious that if my parents had not put their fear aside, I would still be living in Vietnam today.

Our parents were convinced of what life would be like for us if we were to stay in Vietnam: there would be no future. From our home in Vietnam, however, America represented hope and freedom, and my parents were determined to be a part of it. It was that vision of America that gave my parents the strength and the passion to take our first step to the unknown.

Martin Luther King Jr. said it best: "Take the first step in faith. You don't have to see the whole staircase, just take the first step."

Both of my parents have made many sacrifices for us. One of them was to leave their families behind so we could have a better life. They both knew this wasn't an easy task, and there was great risk involved in crossing the border into Cambodia and then Thailand with four little kids. There was a real possibility that we might not survive the trip.

However, both of my parents were fully committed to making this journey. They knew that the risk of staying in Vietnam was far greater.

My mom recruited my older cousin; Bong Tee was seventeen years old at the time. Being the oldest in her family, Bong Tee was both mentally and physically strong, a hard worker, and very dependable. My mom knew my cousin would be capable of helping us along the way. We left Vietnam in the middle of the night and begin our journey by foot to the Cambodian border.

As we made our way through Cambodia's soil, our family

needed to split up so as not to attract any unwanted attention. We did not want to appear to be traveling as a family. My dad traveled with the first group—a band of vendors selling dried fish. Trailing not too far behind the first group was my mom, carrying my five-month-old sister on her side. At the same time, she tied a sheet to my brother's hand and to my hand so that we wouldn't get separated from her. Bong Tee carried my four-year-old sister.

In the middle of our journey, we ran into another group of travelers who were also heading for Thailand. They were local Khmer people. They took just one look at us and knew we weren't local. My mom and cousin were able to speak the Khmer language, but both had a Vietnamese accent. The locals gave my mom and cousin instructions to follow should we meet up with the dreaded Khmer Rouge. Those instructions came just in time.

Shortly after that, we approached a checkpoint. The checkpoint was guarded by half a dozen men with rifles and shotguns. These men were the Khmer Rouge, and they didn't look friendly. They demanded money, jewelry, and other valuables before they would let anyone through. I saw people literally strip to their underwear to show the soldiers that they didn't have anything of value on them.

After taking their tribute, the soldier let the people through one by one.

When our family's turn came, one soldier eyed us up and down. Perhaps this was because of our skin color, which was much lighter than the locals. My mom had warned us earlier that if we were spoken to, we were to keep our mouths shut. She didn't want them to know we were from Vietnam.

My mom and cousin tried hard to blend in with the locals by acting casual and speaking in their accented Khmer.

One of the soldiers asked where she was from and if we were Vietnamese. My mom told him we were not Vietnamese— we were Khmer. He demanded that she hand over anything of value. My mom didn't have much. She gave him the few pieces of the jewelry she had on her. Not satisfied with what she gave him, he went around and checked each and every one of her kids to make sure we weren't carrying any valuables on us.

The soldiers waved through my mom and cousin, who were carrying my younger sisters. Wanna and I stood there, two young boys, afraid. They kept Wanna and me behind. Can you imagine as a parent knowing that you have come this far and now were about to be separated? We were at the point of no return. My dad, with the group in front of us, had no idea what was taking place fifty yards behind him. He could only hope that the solider let us through the checkpoint like they did for him and his group. The plan was already laid out that whatever happened he needed to keep on moving or he would risk getting killed along with everyone else in his group.

Either we were all going through the checkpoint, or we were all going to die at the checkpoint.

Unwilling to give up, my mom begged and pleaded with the soldier to no avail. In my mind, I didn't think this solider was old enough to have his own child. He didn't know what it was like to lose a child. Or maybe he did, and that is why he held us back. Tired of hearing my mom crying and knowing she was not going to back down, one of the soldiers pulled out his handgun and let out three shots. *Bam! Bam! Bam!* At that moment, it seemed as if time was standing still. I can no longer hear the sound coming out of my mom's mouth; I can see her screaming, mouth open, as if everything was in slow motion. All three shots missed Mom by a fraction of an inch. The first shot took out pieces of her long black hair. The last two put a hole through her shirt. You can say someone was watching over my family, three bullets brushing by Mom like the wind. A few of the locals rushed over and dragged my mom away. I don't know if they were worried for my mom's life or if they were more concerned about their own. As the young men dragged my mom away, I was quick to reach my hand out to her, hoping she would pull me with her. Nevertheless, the soldier overpowered my strength. I couldn't break free. All my brother and I could do was watch as our family drifted farther and farther from our sight. Thousands of miles away from home, we were now divided: my brother Wanna and me, our life determined by half a dozen solders who took no prisoners, who cared more about money and smoking their cheap cigarettes. They could easily have killed us with a pull of the trigger. I already mentioned this story early on. It was a defining moment in my life and my parents' lives. It was a time where we were separated; there was a real fear that we would never see each other again. As a child, it was terrifying. I can't imagine what it was like for my mother.

When my mother finally reached us, my brother and I were waiting in a cage like animals in captivity. The mixture of pain, sorrow, and joy was displayed on my mom's face.

For two months, we had been away from our family. Once we were reunited with our mom, she told us that if we had not stopped walking and had continued along the path for just another half a mile, we would have found her and the rest of the group. The group of refugees had been camping a short distance away and were waiting for us.

My brother and I had come up short. We couldn't see what was just ahead of us. If we had only known, we would have kept pushing. The fear of uncertainty is what stopped my brother and me from reaching our family. We had simply given up. We knew what was waiting for us back at the checkpoint—or at least had an idea. What we didn't know was what lay ahead, so we took the path of least resistance, or so we thought.

The path of least resistance is the way our brains are designed. Everything we do in our lives is governed by our past experiences and actions. Essentially, our brains are telling us that we don't want change. We want to drive to and from work the exact same way. We want to brush our teeth the same way. We want to eat sunflower seeds the same way; we dine in the same restaurant and order the same item on the menu. Our brains are computers designed to use past experiences in order to make future decisions. We don't often go against our brains' orders.

The path of least resistance is not a bad thing. In fact, in most situations, it will protect us from harming ourselves. But it also allows for complacency, which inhibits us from wanting to change. In order to achieve our goals, we need to step away from that path of least resistance and come face-to-face with our challenges. Facing our fears and challenges is a difficult thing to do, but we can do it. In fact, we can train our minds to think in a way in which we overcome our fear of change.

The first step in overcoming the path of least resistance is to recognize that this way of thinking slows down your ability to achieve your goal. It limits your capacity to think with a creative mind—or a term you may hear more in the business world, *thinking outside the box.*

The five goals you have already decided to focus your energy on in the next five years are wrought with challenges. Each one will have its own obstacles. However, if you address them as you always have, you will never achieve your objective. You need to think as if you are prepared to change, and in order to do that, you need to prepare to change. You need to mentally start preparing your mind to accept change. This can be done through consistent practice and always looking for opportunities to change yourself and the ways you do things. Below are three ways to start training your mind to think differently and accept the changes you will soon be trying to implement within your transformation.

Expand Your Memory

This is an area I strongly recommend, not only because you are teaching yourself to accept changes but because you are expanding your knowledge of the world around you and dipping into creative thought. This is an area of simple change. Read a book by a new author. Randomly listen to music or artists you've never heard of before. Go to a type of movie you would never have gone to before. This doesn't seem like something that would be hard to do. But imagine if the only movies you watch are science-fiction adventures, and then you go to a cutesy romance. These are simple methods that help you slowly break out of your comfort zone and accept changes. The more you are willing to accept a change, the easier it will be for you to break out of the path of least resistance. You lose the fear that change brings with it.

This will teach your brain different experiences from different perspectives, and you will begin to pull from those experiences in making future decisions.

The Other Point of View

The other point of view is what you do when you come across a situation that needs a decision. You know what your decision would be, but what if you look around the room and see someone else who you know would make a different decision? What would that decision be? Why would he or she make that decision? If you can, address that situation using the other person's decision.

Change Your Collaborators

My friend the tennis player told me the one thing that changed his tennis game for the better. It was only one thing, but it practically changed everything about him, turning him from an average to above-average player. He moved from Wisconsin to Mississippi. Why did this make him a better player? He'd become so stagnant in his game and the people he played. He knew everything about the other players and was never challenged. As soon as he moved, he found a new group of players with all different skill sets.

Similarly, in your life, think of the friends you spend the most time with. It's often that people hang out with like-minded people. Ernest Hemingway was known to hang out (drink) with fascinating people from all walks of life. Why did he do this? He wanted to understand why one person would throw a punch while another would buy someone a drink. By hanging out with people who all had different personalities, he became accustomed to the many perspectives people have. You have the ability to do the same. You don't need to get rid of your friends, but you can look into joining a group or club where you will meet interesting new people with whom you don't share much in common. So the question is, *is the path of least resistance laziness*? I'm sure some will argue that it is, but I don't know if I agree with that statement. The path of least resistance is certainly a more comfortable path for most people, but you can also work very hard on tasks you are comfortable with. Being comfortable with something isn't a bad thing; it is just a safe thing. Change can be scary, but it is necessary, and for most, change is not nearly as difficult as it at first seems.

The path of least resistance can be an easy one . . . at first. But remember that rarely can one skate through life living like this. There was a time in my life when I took the path of least resistance all the time. It wasn't because I was a bad person; I simply didn't want to deal with something. Take, for example, paying the bills. If my bills amount to $800 a month, I could manageably pay that off. However, if I didn't feel like paying my bills one month because it was easier to not pay them, my bills would be $1,600 for the two months. This is a much less manageable way to live. This is the point when you begin to lose the essentials of life, such as electricity, gas, or your house.

Einstein is often credited as saying if you keep doing things the same way over and over again, you'll keep getting the same results. This speaks volumes to those who are habitual procrastinators. If you insist on procrastinating or throwing your bills behind the couch (out of sight, out of mind), then you will face the consequences in the future.

Stepping outside the box and regularly changing your routine will inevitably lead to redirecting your path. You will find that what was once least resistance is now the obstacle that was obviously holding you back. If you don't like the direction your life is going—financial hardships, a job you dislike, friends who pull you down—it's time you change your ways and look down the path that seems dark but in the end may open up into a bright field. I'm not going to tell you this path is easier—and at first, it is certainly not. But as you become accustomed to taking a path better for you, your results will likely improve.

Whatever your goal, seek a way to improve. You don't need to take big steps, but you need to take steps in the right direction. If weight loss is your goal, you don't want to starve yourself. Perhaps you can start monitoring how many steps you take in a day. Then increase that about by two thousand steps each week until you can walk ten thousand steps a day every day. That's almost five miles a day and between 350–600 calories burned a day.

I had a friend with credit card problems. We've talked about financial problems many times so far in this book, and I've offered some good advice. Nevertheless, people need to evaluate their own situations and see what works for them. Well, my friend knew he couldn't lock his credit cards up in a safe or leave them in a drawer away from his wallet because the access was just as easy as grabbing his wallet. What he did— and at the time, I thought this was genius—was he froze the cards in a one-foot-by-one-foot block of ice. I don't know how, but he managed to freeze all those cards directly in the center of the block. Suddenly, he had money he'd never had before. Why? He made it harder to use his cards than whatever he wanted to buy was worth. Any purchase he wanted to make meant having to go home and thaw out that block of ice. Not only did he have to put a lot of working into getting the cards, but this also gave him time to think about whether or not he wanted to make the purchase. For him, this worked wonders. You need to take your notes from the first chapters and determine a plan of action that will work for you.

One of the greatest things about stepping off the path of least resistance is the number of opportunities that come your way by doing so. It will be like opening the door to an entirely new world. In addition, you will learn how to better understand the people around you and why they made their own decisions. Be open to sharing your story, and you will see that your situation is not as unique as you'd thought, and you may in fact learn how others stepped out of their paths or improved their lives.

It is hard to change, but you can do it. Look how far you've gotten in this book. Look at your notes on activities we've discussed.

Remember in chapter 1, I brought up the acronym HOPE. I want you to think about that now. I want you to think about the potential opportunities that open up by opening yourself up to change. Think about the *happiness* you will have with a better life, the *opportunities* that will come to you, the *prosperity* these opportunities will bring, and the *enjoyment* of celebrating your new life.

Chapter 6 Review and Lesson Plan

Following the path of least resistance is a natural-born trait that everyone shares. Whenever we come to an obstacle, it is common for human beings to try to find an easier route around that obstacle even if that means in the future we will have to face harsher consequences. This chapter is about training yourself how to step out of the path of least resistance and challenge yourself. Remember, it is easier to not pay your bills than it is to pay them, but if you don't pay your bills, you run into trouble.

It is the fear of the unknown that leads many of us to the path of least resistance.

An exercise for this chapter is to look at each of your goals and use the three techniques to help you evaluate and look deeper into them.

1. Expand your memory.

2. View your goal from another point of view.

3. Change your collaborators.

In trying to find out how you will achieve your goal, you must find out why you would take the path of least resistance and how to avoid doing that, if possible.

CHAPTER 7

Momentum

Passion is the fuel that ignites the fire.

—Wanny Huynh

My story of change began by opening up a notebook and taking notes on what I wanted in life and why I wasn't getting those things. While I did not see immediate success in this, I did eventually find success. That is the defining point in my life where *the change* took effect. That was the moment I began to build momentum for myself. Even if I had put down that notebook and never worked from it again, it would still have been that momentum change. This is because anytime I felt down, out of luck, no money, or whatever the issue, I could remember back to that time. I could remember how I felt then, and I could remember trying to make a change.

In 2011, the Saint Louis Cardinals had one of the most miraculous runs to win the World Series. They were 10½ games out of first place with a month to play. They got into the playoffs on a win during their last game of the year. They went through the playoffs with one comeback after another. Critical hits, pitching, and plays stunned the country as this seemingly average team always managed to finish on top. It was amazing. Yet almost from the beginning, it was understood these Cardinals were going to win it all. It all started with their run to the postseason and the miracle number of wins they conjured up in September. That was their momentum into the postseason. An average (and sometimes below-average) team during the regular season used momentum to win the World Series. They weren't always on a high, but they always found a way to get back there. That is what I am talking about when I mean momentum.

One thing I've noticed is that everyone assumes change is going to be easy. In the previous chapter, we talked about taking the path of least resistance. I'm sure as you were reading, you at one point thought, *Well, if it is that easy, I would be skinny, wealthy, and not getting a divorce . . .* It's true that change can be difficult. When people come up with a difficult challenge, often the first thought is to simply quit. Apply this thought to momentum. A common fallacy is that momentum has no failure while it is building; the failure comes at the beginning, and it is overcoming that obstacle that drives the momentum. But this isn't true. Momentum has its ups and downs like anything else. Let's look back at the 2011 Saint Louis Cardinals again. Once they got to the postseason, they started to build momentum, and anyone watching them knew something special would happen. That something special happened in game six of the World Series. Game six is referred to by many as the best World Series game of all time. The first six innings were relatively boring, but the last five were some of the greatest baseball any living person has ever seen. While the Cardinals came into the game with momentum and some great games, during this game, they needed to come back five times. In the ninth inning, they were down to their last strike when David Freese hit a triple, allowing a runner to score and tie the game. Then again in the tenth inning, they were down when Lance Berkman hit a double to tie the game. Then in the eleventh inning, David Freese was at the plate again with the game tied. He drilled a homerun to win it. This game, and the entire Cardinals run, is what momentum is about. It was always there, but they were often down and had to pull things together—use their momentum—to step out of the slump.

I can equate this to my own life, taking the story of myself as a child when my brother and I were taken essentially as slaves. My parents' decision, while at the same time scary, was also exciting. This would have been the driver for momentum. Something they may have thought about for years was finally happening. Then the momentum failed when my brother and I were taken at the checkpoint. Our parents searched for us, and when the trader found my mother, the momentum was back. There was then yet another obstacle with the woman who would not let us go without payment. My mother had to somehow come up with the money. She did, and she bought our freedom, propelling us to America. The momentum was always there, but struggle was needed to keep it moving along. Our life in America was similar. It was fraught with ups and downs, some lasting more than others. But with small successes came bigger victories.

When I came to America, life was much different from how it is now. There was no Internet or smartphones. Many jobs that exist now hadn't been thought of then. In a technological world where we would expect life to be easier, what we find is that more options create more problems. One of the greatest challenges we face in our generation is the ability to sustain success. There was a time in America when a person got a job at eighteen, stayed with the company for the next forty-seven years, and then retired. More recent job statistics report the average person will make five to seven career changes in his or her lifetime. These are *career* changes, not *job* changes. It is expected that by the age of forty-two, an average worker may have had ten job changes, which is amazing considering that at forty-two he or she will still have twenty-three years left until retirement age. Statistics for the millennial generation are even more staggering, with many people changing jobs every twelve months. With all these career and job changes in your life, it seems as though it may be impossible to maintain a degree of momentum.

Regardless of your goal in life or why you are reading this book, it should not go without saying that these momentum shifts are built into our being. For thousands of years, humans have been told for every up there must be a down. You may get a raise, and then you may be laid off. You may lose a lot of weight on the Atkins Diet, but you are bound to gain it all back and maybe more. We come by this naturally and accept this as inevitable. What is happening is that once someone has momentum, they stop what it was that brought them the momentum. The opportunities that open up for you are no longer your guideposts. Instead, people will often sit back in the safety of normalcy and allow new opportunities to pass them by. Take going to the gym, for example. When you work out, do you feel great afterward? Do you feel a sense of accomplishment? Do you feel a sense of pride? We all experience that. Isn't it easier to talk yourself out of going? Once you are at the gym and start feeling the sweat running down your neck and your face, aren't you glad you didn't listen to yourself? Once you begin to feel and look good, you begin to build that forward momentum, you want to keep looking and feeling good. Therefore, you go every chance you get. What happens when you miss a few days? You feel a sense of guilt creeping up. On the other hand, isn't it easier to make excuses for yourself, giving you a reason not to go? Next thing you know, one day turns into one week, and one week turns into one month away from the gym. This is what I call a backward momentum. Strive for a forward momentum. You will feel and look good in the long run, and you will be glad you stuck with it.

Weakness as a Strength

Inside every one of us is the ability to do whatever we want with our lives. Everyone struggles through daily life in one way or another. It's what you do with it that counts. Rather than comparing yourself to others, focus within and find your strength and lean toward it. Use your weaknesses to your advantage rather than seeing them as handicaps. One of the best ways to use your weaknesses is to know them and try to define how you can overcome them.

Let's say your goal is to lose thirty pounds. Maybe you don't have time to exercise, so you try to lose weight by calorie reduction. If you try a crash diet or starving yourself, it may work initially, but as soon as you lose your desired weight, you are likely to gain it back again. The aggressiveness and short duration of that weight loss, while it may have seemed effective, was in actuality worse than if you had done nothing. The time you spent losing the weight was momentum, but the time you spent gaining the weight back was demotivating. Aggressive calorie reduction may not work. At the same time, if you do nothing except think of ways to lose weight, then you will also not lose weight. So let's look at the 80/20 rule. The 80/20 rule is a way to manage your goals without going cold turkey. If you take your weakness—let's say cheesecake for this example—and use it as a motivator rather than a staple, you may in fact be able to have your cake and eat it too. Your motivation is to lose weight, your momentum is the weight being lost, and your driver is the cheesecake. Prior to using the 80/20 rule, you may have been eating unhealthy meals 70 percent of the time. With the 80/20 rule, you try to eat 80 percent of your meals as healthy, and 20 percent may be modest desserts or something a little fatter. The reason that 20 percent is important is that you will have cravings. As long as your body knows those cravings will soon be satisfied, the easier it is for you to consistently eat well the other 80 percent of the time. One way you can achieve this goal is to allow yourself a "bad" meal once a week or cheesecake for dessert on Sundays only. Many people will have a single, small piece of chocolate after dinner instead of a bowl of ice cream. It will satisfy your sweet tooth and keep the calories down. The idea is to get in the mind-set of sustaining your goal. If sweets are your weakness, use them to motivate you and continue your momentum instead of allowing them to take you down.

It is the same for any goal. If your goal is to save money, make sure you are also giving yourself the occasional gift to spend money. If your goal is to pass medical school, treat yourself to a day away from studying once in a while.

Using the examples above, I would like you to take the weaknesses identified in previous chapters that would act as obstacles in your personal goal. List at least three. For each weakness you have listed, I want you to write at least two examples of how you would use that weakness to your advantage in achieving your goal. It would look something like this:

Goal: Lose thirty pounds

Weakness: Cheesecake

How this will help me achieve my goal: I will have a two-ounce slice of cheesecake on Sunday nights if I have lost two pounds this week.

Weakness: Chocolate

How this will help me achieve my goal: I will have a milk chocolate Dove candy after dinner each night. This will be my only candy each day.

Weakness: Overeating at each meal

How this will help me achieve my goal: Instead of eating three massive meals each day, I will break my meals up into five to six smaller meals throughout the day.

Focusing on Your Strengths

Once I realized I wanted to become a speaker, I knew my English would be a problem. That is an area I am constantly working on. Another area of weakness was lack of know-how. I didn't know where to start to become a speaker. Rather than focusing on my weaknesses, I sought to improve on them by using one of my strengths, which is my ability to research. Research for me is a motivational tool. I began going to the library and checking out every book and audio CD I could find that would help me improve on these two weaknesses. It was through that process I was able to discover Jack Canfield's book *The Success Principles*. In it, Jack recommended that if I want to become a speaker, join Toastmasters. Research provided the momentum I needed to keep seeking out my goals. The more research I did, the more willing I was to take this new opportunity. I sought out Toastmasters and now am a successful member gaining knowledge and experience. I now have the confidence I need to develop and sustain a speaking career.

As we did in the previous section, I'd like you to list three strengths you do have and how can you use them to stay consistently motivated. For example, if you want to lose that thirty pounds and one of your strengths is that you love to cook, then perhaps you can use that to develop tasty and healthy meals.

Attitude and Persistence

In my journey, I've had two goals: financial freedom and success as a speaker. In both areas, there were times I wanted to give up. Financially, it was an internal struggle with my own habits. As a speaker, I came across naysayers who told me I couldn't do it. Once I developed the confidence to know I was good enough, my self-doubt dissipated. There will always be naysayers and bumps in the road. There will be financial setbacks and unexpected events. Some of those obstacles we create ourselves, such as many of my financial problems. It can be easy to give up. However, what you are doing now, reading my book and taking notes, is a good way to keep your motivation during the hard times. If you started your journey to a new life three months ago and have been doing well, don't let a single setback ruin all your hard work. Look back at the notes you've taken while reading this book. Remember when you first started and how difficult everything seemed. Look through your obstacles, your weaknesses and strengths, and the ways you identified to overcome them. When I look back, I am inspired by my notes. They put a smile on my face at how much I have learned and grown. Use your experiences as laughing points. Have you ever had your car break down in the worst possible place, such as an intersection? At the time, it was probably miserable. You may have used a couple of choice four-letter words. A year later, you find yourself telling that same story, but this time you are laughing about it. Comedy is a great motivator to keep you positive. Use your obstacles as positive mental notes. There's a saying in Minnesota, "If you get caught in a snowstorm, make a snow angel." Or, "If you have a bucket of lemons, make lemonade."

Obstacles will meet you on your path to success. Keep your chin up, be persistent, and always remember to stay positive.

Chapter 7 Review and Lesson Plan

Momentum is what gives you incentive to move forward. For every goal, regardless how small or how big it is, you need incentive to achieve it. If you want to lose thirty pounds, you set smaller goals of perhaps five pounds each. Every time you lose five pounds, that is the incentive telling your mind that you are moving in the right direction and can achieve your goal. Without having momentum, you are likely to give up on your ultimate goal.

In previous chapters, I had you write down some of your flaws and weaknesses. Take at least three of those flaws and write at least two examples for each on how you can use this flaw as an advantage in achieving your goal.

The second exercise is to take those same flaws and write down how you can use your personal strengths to your advantage in overcoming your flaws.

CHAPTER 8

Persistence

Energy and persistence conquer all things.

—BENJAMIN FRANKLIN

Persistence is the ability to continue to get up no matter how many times you've been knocked down. One of my greatest challenges prior to evaluating my life was persistence. As much as I wanted something, I would allow my self-doubts to overcome my desire to succeed. While I always continued to try, I lacked the focus to stay in one direction. Persistence requires willpower to stay on course and flexibility to adapt to unexpected changes and obstacles. It will require determination and the desire to attain your goal. All these factors are the foundation to persistence.

Think of successful people you know, such as Steve Jobs, Bill Clinton, or J. K. Rowling. These, among millions of others, are considered successful, and they all had one thing to link them: the persistence to achieve their goals.

The attributes above are characteristics you will eventually gain if you do not already have them, but in this chapter, I want to focus on two subjects that will not only help you gain the characteristics above but will also help you in learning how to become persistent. Those two things are facing your fears and building a commitment to learning and growing.

Facing Your Fears

In chapter 6, I talked about facing your fears and related it to my parents and our departure from Vietnam. Like my parents, in order to achieve your goals, you will need to tackle your fears head on. There is no way around it. Like ignoring your bills, if you do not tackle the issue, then the problem will not go away, and you will not attain your goal. Fear affects our day-to-day lives. Whether you are afraid to talk to a stranger in an elevator or afraid of driving, you will face fears daily. Being afraid is a natural emotion designed to protect us from making poor decisions that can hurt us. However, if we can't overcome some of our fears, there is little hope we will accomplish our dreams.

Open up your notebook and start a new section labeled *Overcoming Your Fears*. If you've been keeping notes as you read, this exercise should be easier than the earlier ones. What we hope to do with this exercise is to define your fears and discover how to overcome them.

The first step in this exercise is to list as many fears as you can think of. You can use earlier exercises, such as identifying obstacles and weaknesses. How do these fears make you feel? Do they make you feel afraid, nervous, stressed out? Where do they come from? Many people have a fear of dogs because of something that happened when they were younger.

Next, pick one of your fears. From that fear, let's develop

a plan to overcome it. For example, if you are nervous about speaking in front of a group, start by tackling small, manageable tasks. Perhaps you would start by reading from a book out loud in front of a mirror. Then you memorize a short passage from that book and read it out loud as you walk through the house. Take baby steps in building up your confidence. Try to start up short conversations with strangers and make small talk. "Hey, nice weather today. I'd love to be playing tennis. Do you play?" As you slowly begin to gain confidence in speaking to strangers, you could look up a local Toastmasters group. Visit the club and interact with the members. If interested, become an active member.

This is how it works. Tackle one fear at a time and take baby steps until you are comfortable. Don't move on to another step until you are confident in the current one.

Visualize yourself defeating that fear. After all, it is all in the mind, right? Take ten minutes each morning to mentally see yourself overcoming your fear. How does it feel? How does it taste? Mentally seeing yourself taking control of your fear helps you to realize your fear can be overcome. Think about past fears and how you overcame them. Did you have adversity, and how did you address those obstacles?

Throughout this entire book and especially in this exercise, remember that everything can be learned. Remember when you were a kid and the teacher asked what you wanted to be when you grew up? Do you remember your answer? Doctor, lawyer, baseball player, movie star, firefighter . . . As you got older, what happened to those dreams? Why did you stop dreaming as you did when you were younger? Were you afraid of failure? Afraid of what others might think? Were you afraid of hearing "You dream too big" or "You will never achieve that"? Maybe someone even told you were crazy. I have heard all of this and more. Remember this is your dream you are living, not someone else's.

When I truly understood this, I stopped caring about what others thought and how they viewed me. When you remove the limitations people impose on you, you will be more open to try new ideas. Nothing great comes from this realization if we don't overcome the fears that stop us from achieving our goals.

Commit to Learning and Growing

Champion athletes know what it takes to win. Learning is an ongoing journey; fuel your mind with new ideas. To be a champ, you need to equip yourself with tools, books, and other forms of learning that help move you to achieve greater results. The champ knows there is always room to improve, and they never stop learning.

Gather as much knowledge as you can, and become an expert in your field. I can sit here and tell you to read, read, read, but that is not the only way to learn. Take classes, and join clubs. Focus on things you do right and things you can improve on—a small exercise in learning and growing. For one week, I would like you to sit down at the end of the day and jot down a couple of things that happened to you earlier in the day that could have gone better. Then write a couple of sentences on what you could have done to improve on the situation and what you think the result would be.

The reason I ask you to do this is because the next time you are in a similar situation, you will remember the other experience and know how to handle it better. This is a learning technique. It's something that you can use to improve yourself in real life.

Another technique you can use is to jot down a few notes for the upcoming day on what you think you will accomplish or do. It's kind of a to-do list for yourself. At the end of the day, ask yourself what you did not complete. Then write down why you didn't complete the task and what you could have changed in your day to have completed it.

As you progress with either or both of these exercises, you will find that you are not only motivating yourself to handle situations better and complete your task list but you are also learning from personal experiences.

Remember, persistence is the ability to continue to get up despite the number of times you are knocked down. Keep your vision clear and directed at your goals and as in the prior exercises view your setbacks as life lessons. Write those lessons down and remember them. Mistakes should be thought of as lessons, not failures. The more you see life this way, the better your opportunity for success.

When to Give Up

Yes, you read that section title correctly. Should you never give up? Sometimes it's the best option. It sounds crazy, yes. I've spent several hours or days with you and over thirty thousand words telling you the importance of pushing through obstacles, overcoming fear, and focusing on your objective, and now I am telling you, "Hey, it's okay to give up sometimes." Does this sound a little wishy-washy or like I'm backtracking? Well,

I'm not doing either. So hear me out. *There are times when giving up is the best option.* And you need to treat this as an obstacle and learning experience.

Before you freak out on me, let me give you an example. Have you ever heard of a company named Traf-O-Data? If you are a trivia person, maybe, but more than likely you have not. Well, in 1972, Traf-O-Data was the first company started by Bill Gates and Paul Allen. Both Gates and Allen ran Traf-O-Data for a couple of years before realizing it was not going to give them the success they wanted. They gave up and pursued other avenues they felt would be more profitable. Think Microsoft.

So when should you give up? Think of it this way: as you go after your goals, they may change. Sometimes life obstacles force change. Sometimes you grow in a different direction. You should never cling to a goal that won't inspire you. If I am pursuing a goal of being a public speaker and spend a year in the pursuit only to find out I don't enjoy it, I would be off my rocker to continue. Sure, I may have spent a year learning a new trade, but if I don't want to do it, the longer I force myself to continue on without a clear goal I want to pursue, the more time I waste when I could be applying myself to other pursuits.

Sometimes I think about my short-lived career in real estate. I enjoyed it, but I wouldn't say it was my career path. Despite the market crash, for me at the time, it was perhaps not the best thing. Selling real estate is dependent upon sales. If I don't sell, I don't eat. While I tend to sometimes take the riskier path, I do realize that I also need stability to maintain my personal goals. That's what I did. I found a stable job I love, which gives me the opportunity to go after my personal goals.

So don't be afraid to give up, but only if you have a good

reason. Ask yourself why you were going after your goal and if that goal still means something to you. Admittedly, it is easier to give up than to persist with something you don't enjoy. If that is the option you choose, please make sure you have thought long about it. There is a fine line between giving up and being frustrated.

Chapter 8 Review and Lesson Plan

Persistence is your personal drive to keep going. You can have all the momentum in the world, but without persistence, you can just as easily give up on your goal. In this chapter, we discussed ways to stay persistent in your objectives.

Exercise 1: List your fears. List as many as you can.

Exercise 2: Pick one of your fears and develop a plan to overcome that fear by using smaller steps. If you need to, review the example about the fear of talking in front of a group.

Exercise 3: The next time you think you could have done something better, take a small break and then rethink yourself through that situation. Write a couple of notes on how you could have responded better to the situation and what you think the results would have been had you acted differently.

Exercise 4: Make a list of the tasks you want to complete in a day. At the end of the day, reevaluate your list. What did you accomplish, and what did you not accomplish? For the tasks you were not able to complete, why did you not complete them? What could you have changed in your day that would have helped you complete all your tasks?

CHAPTER 9

Overcoming Criticism

*The problem with most of us is that we would rather be
ruined by praise than saved by criticism.*

—NORMAN VINCENT PEALE

When I was growing up in America, I was afraid of how I was judged. Because of this, I began to act, speak, and dress in a certain way. I became the people who I admired most in my life. For me, that would be my friends and family. For a long time, I admired them because I thought they were better than I was. However, as I grew older, I began to reevaluate those I looked up to. I realized that they were not better than I was, and they were not smarter than I was. I was acting and dressing the same as they were because it was expected that I would do so. While I still admired my friends and family, I began to seek out other people who I admired and respected, most of whom were in the business world. I began to pick and choose my friends. I remember in my teenage years, my dad said something to me that I have never forgotten.

He said, "Son, don't have too many friends." Back then,

I didn't know what he meant, but as I got older, it became clearer. The more friends and people I associated with, the more influenced I would become. You become the person you hang out with. The statement is clear in my mind. As I look back, I realize the impact his words made on me. My dad was simply warning me to pick and choose whom I surrounded myself with. He didn't say not to make friends but to be careful of who I chose to take advice and ideas from. They can, and will, impact your behavior.

There will be times that you will find criticism in your social group. Often, this will occur for the very reason I just mentioned. If you are not following the norm, then you are often an outsider.

The Greek stoic philosopher Epictetus once said, "If you want to improve, be content to be thought foolish and stupid." These are words to live by if you hope to step outside your comfort zone and be more than what others believe you can be.

Criticism is not only upsetting but can leave a long-bitter taste in your mouth. Many people will hold decade-long grudges against people who criticized them. However, while being criticized can hurt and make you feel angry, you must remember that it is a part of life, and everyone at some time is criticized. Step one of dealing with criticism is the hardest step. Forgive those who criticize you. You need to remember that, while you hope everyone stands behind you and supports you, you are the one stepping outside the box. You are the one doing something uncomfortable, and therefore you are also making other people feel uncomfortable; that is okay. Looking at criticism from another person's point of view will often show you that the reason you are being scrutinized is not because the person hopes you fail but rather because that person doesn't want to see you fail. What he or she may not realize is that you need to fail in order to succeed.

When someone approaches you, try not to take the criticism personally or immediately put up a defensive stance. In addition, a common reaction would be to try to find fault in the other person. When we become emotional, our ability to think becomes limited, and our reactions are often questionable. By acting emotionally, you will miss the point of the interaction entirely.

One good way of dealing with criticism is thanking the person for his or her opinion and stepping away from the interaction. Go for a walk or bike ride. Do something that will help you think more clearly. Think about what the person said and if he or she was trying to be spiteful or helpful. If this person is trying to be spiteful, it becomes easy to dismiss the comment, although it may still hurt. If he or she is trying to help, it may still hurt, but try to look at the comments from the other person's viewpoint. If you don't think the criticism is warranted, then ignore it, but what you may also find is that there is a degree of advice that, had you been defensive, you may have missed. If you do have an occasion where someone provided helpful criticism, go back to that person. Be sure to acknowledge that you thought about what he or she had said and you want to discuss it further. Not only will this help you mend the hurt you initially felt when the criticism was given, but it may also allow the other person to see your side of things, and by doing this, you may garner a new supporter rather than a critic.

When dealing with naysayers or negative critics, you

will find that this can be the most difficult criticism to deal with. Often, negative critics harbor bad feelings toward you, purposely are trying to hurt you, or have a sense of jealousy that you are reaching for something they either can't or are afraid to go for.

Regardless of such intent, the words shared will often be brash and difficult to hear and deal with. You will think of them often in the next few days, weeks, months, and even years. These words can develop an animosity that could last a lifetime. Unfortunately, because it is so difficult, you end up losing in the end. You could have lost a good friend or become detached from a family member because of your inability to put those comments behind you. I think back on myself and wonder if this has ever happened. I'm sure it has, although I can't recall with whom. Have you ever heard the expression, "Don't burn your bridges"? That expression can relate directly to criticism. My goal in life is to help people. I want them to know that they have a chance in life, regardless of their current position. I want you to sit back and reflect on your life and who you are and to know you can achieve your dreams when you finish this book. So what good would it do me if I were to become emotional and upset every time I was criticized? Maybe I would act irrationally and stop talking to the person. Maybe I would lose a good friend. Or, worse, maybe I would lose the ability to help someone in the future because of a poor reaction to honest criticism. It's simply not worth it.

One of the best words of advice is from the Dalai Lama: *Will it matter a year from now*? This is something I've repeated to myself many times. For every negative interaction I've had, for every time I have been hurt, and for each criticism, I ask myself how, in a year from now, that criticism will affect me. It takes a little time to work, but try it. When someone criticizes you, ask yourself the same question. "In a year from now, will my life have been changed because of what that person said?" The answer is way more often *no* than it is *yes*.

Criticism, hurtful or helpful, is something you can learn from. Use someone else's words as a teaching tool for yourself. Use that experience to benefit you in the future.

Chapter 9 Review and Lesson Plan

Criticism is something everyone faces, especially if you plan to step outside the normal, and in order to achieve your goals, it is likely you will need to step outside the norm. Criticism can be hurtful, painful, cruel, and, in many circumstances, demotivating. In this chapter, we talk about how you handle criticism and techniques where you can take criticism and use it to your favor.

There are two exercises in this chapter, but they may not both pertain to your situation. If one does not pertain to your situation, then try the one that does, but remember that both are effective in managing criticism.

Exercise 1: If you are given criticism, even if hurtful, evaluate the criticism. Take a break and go for a walk or bike ride. Think about why you were given that criticism. If it was not out of spite, then determine if you can use that criticism to help. Next, approach the person who offered the criticism and thank him or her. Try to look at that person's perspective, and ask questions if you need to.

Exercise 2: This may be easier than the previous exercise and is meant for the criticism that seems like an attack or out of spite. While the hurt and anger may be hard to overlook, ask yourself a question: In a year from now, will this person's words matter to me? More often than not, you will find that what the person had said will mean nothing to you in a year.

CHAPTER 10

Taking Action

Action is the foundational key to all success.

—PABLO PICASSO

If you've gotten this far, you've already started to take action on achieving your goals—that is, for most people, the most difficult challenge in taking control of their lives. But now it is time to take your notes and the planning you've already done in this book and put that plan into action.

You can have the fastest and most powerful car in the world, but it will not take you anywhere if you don't start it up. You can have the greatest tools in the world, but if you don't put them to good use, they are worthless. Taking action is the starting point to achieving any goal you set for yourself. Without action, nothing great in life is ever accomplished. Even if you have mastered all the previous principles in this book, if you do not act on them, all your knowledge will be pointless.

I can take from my own life. I had taken action many times. I'd developed many plans for how I would succeed, get myself out of a rut, and gain wealth. What held me back? It's simple: procrastination.

Time and time again, I failed to act on the things I knew to be true and the things that really mattered the most to me.

Because of my parents' determination, courage, and sacrifice, I am now able to live in this land of opportunity. Many of us take that opportunity for granted. We have a wealth of resources surrounding us, if only we can tap into them. It is not where you have been or what has happened to you in the past that matters. What matters most is where you want to go with your life and the resources you have at your disposal to make dreams a reality.

Wealth, success, and happiness begin with a mind-set. You can become anybody you want. You need a desire and passion to achieve your goals.

Goal Setting

Success rarely comes by accident. When runners attempt their first marathon, they often hear the same piece of advice: "Don't compete against other runners; compete against your own time." Marathon runners are the epitome of goal setters. The marathon is a race that lasts between two hours for the elite runners and up to seven hours for recreational marathoners. But the race takes six months to years of preparation. What the runners learn early on is to pace their mile times. The entire race is dependent upon these mile paces. As you watch a marathon, you will notice runners looking at their watches often. This is to compare their pace with their goal pace. If they are running too slow, they may speed up, and if they are running too fast, they may slow down. Goal setting for a runner begins from the first day they begin training for the marathon. The ultimate goal is to finish the marathon at a certain time, but it is the goal setting leading up to the event that is most important. Each day is planned as to how far or for how long the runner will run. Rest days are planned. Sprint days are planned. And for many, meals are planned. The reason why this is done is because a marathon is a long race that needs preparation.

Like your personal goals, it will take a long time to achieve. If your goal is to raise your credit score from 520 to 750, this will take time. You will need to plan your credit payments and usage and ensure bills are paid in time—and that you are not spending beyond 20 percent of your available credit. You will need to have a budget to avoid overspending. You may have to seek out new lines of credit. But a plan needs to be put together in order for you to achieve your goal.

Developing goals is important in any endeavor. But a goal like *I want to complete this marathon* or *I want a 750 credit score* will not get you where you need to be. Having an ultimate goal, which is what both of those are, is great and needed. But goal setting is really the process of putting together a series of attainable goals, short goals to propel you forward and help you feel as if you are accomplishing something.

The November 1981 issue of *Management Review* contained a paper by George T. Doran called "There's a S.M.A.R.T. Way to Write Management's Goals and Objectives." While this style of goal setting is directed at business—specifically management—the format can be applied to personal goals, as well. SMART goals stand for:

Specific: A specific goal defining the five *W*s. *What* do I want to accomplish? *Why* do I want to accomplish this goal? It refers to specific reasons like the purpose or benefits of achieving this goal. *Who*—for example, will you be the only person working on this goal, or will others be helping? Will you hire a financial consultant? Or perhaps, if training a marathon, will you run with a running club? *Where* will the goal take place? *Which* are any requirements or restraints you may have?

Measurable: How will you measure your goal? You should be able to make the goal quantifiable. What credit score do you want? How much weight do you want to lose, or what do you want to weigh? How much money do you want to have in a bank account? If you cannot quantify the goal, then you will need at least a well-defined qualitative goal so that you can say, "This goal has been clearly achieved," when you have accomplished it.

Attainable: Answers the question of how the goal can be accomplished and whether it is realistic based on your personal constraints. Goals should push you and will likely be difficult, but they should not be extreme or impossible. For example, if you are running your first marathon and are a beginning runner, a four-hour finish time is difficult yet realistic. A two-hour finish time is extreme.

Realistic: Is this a goal you can achieve? This isn't necessarily answering the question of whether or not you can attain the goal but refers more to the relevance of the goal to either your ultimate goal or your personal being. For example, if you set a goal of fifty jumping jacks a day as part of an ultimate goal of running a marathon, you should ask yourself, *Is this goal relevant to being able to run a marathon*? It may be a goal, but if you didn't have it, could you still attain your ultimate goal?

Time: Answers the question of when you will be able to attain the goal or when you can achieve a series of smaller goals and how long it will take to attain them. If your ultimate goal is to have a 750 credit score, your goal setting will likely have several points in between where you are and that eventual 750. Perhaps you will give yourself six months to have a score of 625 and ten months to have a score of 660.

Defining SMART goals is essential to achieving your ultimate goals. In order to define your goals, I would like you to first list your ultimate goal; for example, "I would like to have a 750 Experian credit score by December of 20XX." Knowing your ultimate goal is important, but how you get there is more important. What I want you to do next is try to list out as many goals as you can think of that will get you to your ultimate goal. For this example, you can list things like "Pay off my credit cards," "Use between 10 percent and 20 percent of my available credit every month," "Pay off my bills on time every month," and "Acquire a car loan." Once you have exhausted your list, I would like you to review each goal and turn it into a SMART goal. Once you have done that, prioritize your goals. You can prioritize however you see fit as long as you have a logical means to it, such as "This goal I can accomplish in two months, and these I can accomplish in ten months."

After you have your goals in order, you can develop your game plan if you don't already have one.

While goal setting takes time—and should take a fair amount of it—it is worth it in the end. But don't let this initial goal-setting work be put aside and go untouched. There will likely be obstacles in your path that you hadn't accounted for in your initial plans. That is okay. Goals should have a degree of flexibility. If you are training for a marathon, you may get sick or have an injury. If you are attempting to improve your credit, you may lose your job. It is okay to modify your goals as you work your way to your ultimate goal. Do not think that if you miss a goal or cannot attain a goal within a specific time that you should abandon your objective. Keep that ultimate goal in mind and adapt your smaller goals to fit your current situation. A goal should be flexible and revisited often. As you start taking action on completing your goals, evaluate the goals you are working on. Define the frequency—for example, every Sunday. Ask yourself where you are with your goal, if the goal still attainable, or if obstacles have changed your ability to complete the goal on time. If you need to modify your goal, feel free to. Keep in mind that goals should be more difficult to attain than doing little or nothing. A goal should not be modified because you are procrastinating or because you are spending too much time watching TV in the evening. You should have a legitimate reason for modifying your goal and not staying on track.

Goal setting is a tool to keep you on track and measure your ability to attain your ultimate goal. When you are done setting your goals, I want you to be able to sit back with a smile on your face knowing you can achieve your ultimate goal. You should be proud of the initial work you have put into attaining your goal, and you should feel excited knowing that you will achieve it.

Chapter 10 Review and Lesson Plan

By now, you should have an ultimate goal and several smaller goals that will keep the momentum going while you try to achieve your life-changing goal.

In this chapter, we talked about SMART goals and how to formulate them, write them, and use them to succeed. Your final exercise is to gather all the goals you have developed up to this point and use them to achieve your ultimate goal. I would like you to turn each goal, big or small, into a SMART goal.

CHAPTER 11

Closure

Fall down seven times, get up eight.

—Japanese proverb

I remember the trip my brother and I had as children. I remember the confusion, pain, and fear of abandonment. For a child, the greatest fear is to be left alone. My brother and I didn't know how long we would be together after we were taken. In fact, it is quite possible that if not for my parents' determination to find us and a stranger who was our guardian angel, my brother and I could have easily been separated after we were taken. The two of us lived the life of so many other children shortly after the Vietnam War. We were, for a short period of time, given the opportunity to taste the pain of slavery, of fear, and of loneliness. Most who were in our shoes never experience life beyond that. Many children to this day die within these confines, many remain illiterate, and many are enslaved by the loss of their parents. Yet I had the opportunity to come to America and succeed. I had the opportunity to come to America and fail.

Not long ago, I ran into a man after one of my speeches. He pulled me aside and shared with me his story. As a child, he was brought up in a bad neighborhood. Growing up, he got shot at and attacked by gang members. He then made a promise to himself that he would not let his kids go through what he had gone through. Having a game plan, he was able to set a goal for himself and his family. Through hard work and persistence, he was able to move his family to a nicer neighborhood, where his kids can run free without having to worry about drive-by shootings and hanging with the wrong crowd. Once he was done sharing with me his story, he asked if I had ever been shot at. I look at him with a smile and asked, "Do missiles and bombs count?" I went on, "We are living the dream, my friend." We parted. My life and the problems I've had are my problems. While sometimes I was not given a fair opportunity, many of my problems stem from my own actions. Most of us create our own problems in life. To confront our own demons and face our fears is something we all have the opportunity to do yet remain afraid of doing. Yet this is the only way to overcome what we face. I had to overcome my fear of not knowing who I was. I found myself without an identity and trying to find one. All I wanted to do when I was younger was fit in and be a part of something. As I grew, I tried to fit into places I never belonged. These places and the people I befriended were not me. I slowly found my way out, yet I appreciate those friends who stood by me and who I did belong with. They were the ones who helped me through my lack of an identity.

My own demons of procrastination and poor money management worked toward the antithesis of what I wanted to become. To this day, I can't tell you if I knew these were even problems while I dreamed to succeed. Perhaps, at the time, I did not see them as problems—that is, not until I hit bottom.

Regardless of my feelings about my family or friends in different times of my life, I know my problems were my own curse. I know that my success comes from my ability to stand up to my internal struggles and be a better man than I was when I allowed my life to hit bottom. I am lucky to have parents, siblings, friends, and a beautiful wife who support me. I am a man who faced his fears and found himself climbing out of a hole. I am a man who looked up out of that hole and found many willing hands to help me. Fear, misunderstanding, and criticism all played a role in the actions I took when I was younger. Yet when I taught myself to harness those emotions and use them to my benefit, I found my identity.

I am a lucky man, and many people are not as fortunate to be able to make such a statement. In particular, a good friend of mine who can say he had a good family to support him was someone who did not put himself in his own hole. My friend had been diagnosed with leukemia. His story for me is one of inspiration. His is a story of surviving cancer and suddenly finding himself with a new goal in life:

March 9, 2012. It was a Friday, I remember, because I had gone to the doctor earlier in the week because there was something wrong with my body, and I couldn't figure out what it was. At first, the doctor thought it might be an infection of some kind. But then the doctor called Friday and left a message for us to call him back. He wouldn't tell us the problem over the phone, so we went in. Once we got to the hospital and the doctor started to explain what was going on, I couldn't believe it. It was as if I were oblivious to the whole thing, like it wasn't happening. He [the doctor] explained how it affected the body. I was just thinking I could take a pill or something and then go home. But he suggested I go through chemotherapy. I ended up staying at the hospital, in and out for like five months. I ended up having three sessions of chemotherapy, and each session was worse than the other one. It ended up attacking the immune system. It just kills everything, all the good cells and the bad cells. That was why I couldn't be around people, in case they were carrying a sickness. I would go home for a week or two, but then I would get back to the hospital very sick, which was why I was there for a couple of months.

It was a huge impact on my family. I already knew we had a strong bond, but something like this, a sickness, can really prove how strong a family is.

I remember being so confused that first day I found out. I mean, I don't smoke, and I don't drink. I didn't realize why this was happening. Emotionally, I don't think I had any problems until the third week after the first session when my hair started falling out. That's when it really hit me: I have cancer. I had lost one hundred pounds within six weeks.

There was a time the doctors told me that there was a 90 percent chance that I would not make it through the three sessions without getting all the cancer. I was scared. There are pictures of me during a two-week period with tubes down my throat that I don't even remember.

Through it all, my wife was the strong one. She was taking care of the kids and then was back at the hospital with me. It was a busy six months for her. She was the trooper. I just had to lie there and take the medicine.

Life is kind of back to normal, although I did have to make some changes. The big one is I have more family time, which is something I didn't have before. I work-work-worked all the time before, thinking I'd have the chance to hang out with the kids later on when they were older. Now I've taken another position at my company and moved to a different shift so I can be home when my kids get off school. You can never predict what life is going to bring.

This story is important in that it is a constant reminder that life is not always fair, but in the end, it can positively impact yourself and your goals. My friend overworked himself in order to financially provide for his family. His financial goals were not unlike mine. Yet after battling leukemia, his goals quickly changed to spending time with family and realizing that was most important for him.

Life changes, people change, and goals change. This is true until you die. There should not be a time in your life where you stop trying to improve, strengthen, and revisit your goals. You can do whatever you set your mind to. Whether you are trying to be financially secure, lose weight, or recover from a disease, set goals, stay focused, and be persistent, and you will achieve more than you'd ever thought possible. The meaning of life is all about happiness. Are you happy with what you have? If you are not happy, then you are not living life to the fullest. This book is about finding and creating HOPE: happiness, opportunity, prosperity, and enjoyment of life. Thank you for allowing me to share my journey with you. Now it's your turn to make an impact in this world. Share the message of HOPE. I wish you great health, success, and a prosperous year.

Acknowledgments

From the words of John Donne: "Human beings necessarily depend on one another, as in You can't manage this all by yourself, no man is an island." This book would not have been possible if I didn't have a creative team behind me. From my editor, to proofreader, book designer, to my parents who have been very supportive and encouraging with their unconditional love. I wouldn't be where I am today if it wasn't for their sacrifice and determination to risk everything so that I could have the opportunity to chase my dreams. And for that I owe them a great debt of gratitude. May their lives be filled with joy and happiness for many years to come. To my brother and sisters whose love I cannot put into words. Thank you for being there when I needed you. To my mentors, there are just too many to list, you know who you are. You have helped shape me to be the man that I wanted to be.

Catherine Rai Cardenuto, thank you for taking time out of your busy schedule to help go over the manuscript and provide feedback and guidance. Jody Mabry, thank you for your help in bringing this book to life. Alicia Ester, thank you for your guidance throughout the publishing process. My lovely wife Tracy for all of your support and encouragement: thank you for believing in me.

Most of all, my readers, it's you who inspire me to continue writing and sharing my stories.